THE CALL OF THE WILD & WHITE FANG

NOTES

including
- *Life of the Author*
- *General Plot Summaries of Each Novel*
- *List of Characters in Each Novel*
- *Summaries and Commentaries for Each Novel*
- *Critical Theories*
- *Questions for Review*
- *Selected Bibliography*

by
Samuel J. Umland, Ph.D.
University of Nebraska

INCORPORATED
LINCOLN, NEBRASKA 68501

Editor

Gary Carey, M.A.
University of Colorado

Consulting Editor

James L. Roberts, Ph.D.
Department of English
University of Nebraska

ISBN 0-8220-0279-5
© Copyright 1982
by
C. K. Hillegass
All Rights Reserved
Printed in U.S.A.

1991 Printing

Cliffs Notes, Inc.   Lincoln, Nebraska

CONTENTS

JACK LONDON NOTES

LIFE OF THE AUTHOR

Jack London grew up in the slum area of Oakland, California, a place which he later called "the cellar of society." Born out of wedlock on January 12, 1876, he never knew his father, William Henry Chaney, who had left Jack's mother, Flora Wellman, before Jack's birth. On September 7, 1876, Flora Wellman married John London, from whom her son Jack took his name.

By the age of fifteen, London had turned delinquent. Barely seventeen, he signed aboard the schooner *Sophie Sutherland*, bound for Japan and the Bering Sea. Returning from the voyage in 1894, London began to be interested in the plight of the underprivileged and working classes, and so he joined a group of militant workers who were going to Washington to protest the wretched working conditions in the country, caused by the Depression of 1894. He did not reach Washington, however; he deserted this "Industrial Army" in Hannibal, Missouri, and for a time he traveled around the country as a hobo. At Niagara Falls, he was arrested for vagrancy and sentenced to the Erie County Penitentiary. He was released after thirty days, and he quickly caught the first train heading West, arriving eventually in Oakland.

It was probably soon after his release from the penitentiary that London became seriously interested in politics, and as a result, he joined an Oakland branch of the Socialist Labor Party in April, 1896. Then soon afterward, he enrolled as a student at the University of California at Berkeley, where he attempted to further his studies in the most influential scientific and philosophic theories of the late nineteenth century – Darwinism, Social Darwinism, Nietzscheism, and Marxism. He soon became restless, though, and he left the University during his second semester as a student. From California, he went North, to the Klondike to search for gold, and his adventures there became the basis of many stories. In fact, two of his most famous novels, *The Call of the Wild* and *White Fang*, are set in the North, and while these two novels are perhaps his most famous in the United States, London is equally well known in places outside of the United States as the author of a number of socialistic works: *The Iron Heel* (1908), *The War of the Classes* (1905), *Revolution and Other Essays* (1910), and *The People of the Abyss* (1903). London has said that *The People of the Abyss* was his favorite book; it is a sociological study about the worst areas of poverty in London, England's East End and is based on London's first-hand experiences while he lived there.

Early in 1900, London married Bessie Maddern and began his career as a serious writer. He soon finished his first novel, *A Daughter of the Snows*, which was published in 1902, and in the summer of 1903, London met Charmian Kittredge, whom he promptly fell in love with and abruptly left his wife and two daughters for.

Returning to the subject of London's fiction, it is interesting to note that his novel *The Iron Heel* (written in 1906 and published in 1908) belies London's avid interest in science fiction. Considered to be one of his best novels, the novel predicts a Fascist oligarchy in the United States under threat from a proletarian revolution, allegedly pictured in manuscripts discovered by scholars in the socialist twenty-seventh century. "A Thousand Deaths" (1899), London's first science fiction tale, utilizes some key motifs of the science fiction genre: a solitary, embittered scientist subjects his son to some revivification experiments, but the scientist is soon dematerialized by a fantastical weapon invented by his son. London's story "The Shadow and the Flash" (1903) has as its concern the quest for invisibility on the part of two scientists. "The Enemy of All the World" (1908) features a "mad scientist" who invents a formidable weapon and terrorizes the world with it. Much of London's science fiction indicates his belief in the superiority of the white race. In 1904, London visited Japan and other Far Eastern countries, and his correspondences from there disguise his deep racist attitudes toward the Oriental people. For example, at a Socialist rally in Oakland, after his return from the Far East, he publicly declared his hate of the Oriental races, and in his science fiction story "The Unparalleled Invasion" (1910), the West destroys the Chinese with a bacteriological bomb. In London's posthumous novella *The Red One* (1918), London pictured a stone-age society which has formed a death cult and worships a strange sphere from outer space.

Plagued with debts throughout his whole life, London accepted an offer from Macmillan in 1902 for $2,000.00 for *The Call of the*

Wild, which is all of the money that London ever received from what is perhaps his most famous book. In 1904, London decided to compose a "complete antithesis [and] companion piece" to *The Call of the Wild*. Instead of the devolution or the decivilization of a dog, he said, "I'm going to give the evolution, the civilization of a dog. . . ." The result was *White Fang*, which appeared two years later, in 1906. In 1913, London published *John Barleycorn*, a book about his alcoholism, and a book which should be considered as a sincere tract describing the plight of the alcoholic.

In ill health most of his life, by 1915, London was almost lame. His bowels gave him continual pain, and in order to reduce the pain, London began using opium and morphine, and it was not long before he became addicted to the drugs. As a consequence, his kidneys were also eventually wrecked by his misuse of all of the drugs, and London refused to even quit smoking, although he had cancer of the throat. By November 21, 1916, London was in such poor health that he spent the entire day in bed. Then shortly before dawn the next day, he injected himself with what would prove to be an overdose of drugs. That evening, he died; he was forty years old. There is, naturally, some question as to whether his death was an intentional suicide.

While writing for only sixteen years, London produced an amazing body of work: nineteen novels, eighteen books of essays and short stories, and numerous other books, both sociological and autobiographical, and London's popularity has hardly ebbed over the years. *The Call of the Wild* has been translated into more than thirty languages, and it exists in millions of copies; sales and printing of *White Fang* are only slightly less in number than *The Call of the Wild*. Other popular London novels are *Martin Eden* (1909), *The Valley of the Moon* (1913), and the book which many critics feel comes closest to being the Great American Novel, *The Sea Wolf* (1904).

THE CALL OF THE WILD

GENERAL PLOT SUMMARY

Buck, a huge, four-year-old half-Saint Bernard and half-Scottish shepherd dog, is living a life of civilized ease in California's Santa

Clara Valley in the home of Judge Miller. It seems to be the best of all possible worlds, for Buck is the most prized animal that the Judge owns. Around this time, however, gold is discovered in the great North, and large dogs suddenly become tremendously valuable because these types of dogs are needed to haul the heavy sleds through the deep snow fields.

Tragically, for Buck, one of the Judge's servants (an addictive gambler) steals Buck and sells him to a ring of thieves who are making a great deal of money by buying and selling dogs to northern traders. Buck's spirit, however, does not adapt as easily as do some of the other docile big dogs. Buck cannot tolerate being tied up and beaten; he fights against his cruel new master, but all of his efforts to escape are futile. Thus, Buck learns the new concept of "master," even though he learns it reluctantly: a man with a club is a master and must, at all costs, be obeyed.

After days of travel on both train and boat, Buck discovers that he is in the primitive North, and there he rapidly learns to conform to the laws of the primitive new world. For example, he encounters such problems as how to work as a member of a dog team pulling a sled, how to burrow into a hole in the snow in which to sleep, how to survive perpetual hunger pains, and how to rely on his native intelligence and his animal instincts.

Buck also soon learns that the dominant primordial bestial instinct is very strong in him, and he learns just as quickly that when he is attacked, he must take the offensive immediately in order to survive; as a result of this type of living adjustment, Buck also learns that he has to live a life of almost continual alertness, as well as in almost continual pain and discomfort. Yet Buck has one advantage: his size makes him fearful to the other dogs. Still, however, all is far from pleasant, for even though Buck can defend himself quite well and is ever-ready to scrap with another dog, he has a secret that he must keep to himself: because Buck has arrived so recently from civilization, the craggy ice and snow of the North tear at his paws and make his work extremely painful.

After being in constant hunger for many days, Buck's old instinct to kill and eat raw meat and warm blood is rekindled within him. About this same time, Buck is constantly pitted against another powerful dog, Spitz, the lead dog of his sled team. After several skirmishes with Spitz, Buck's decisive fight with him occurs, and the result of the fight is a victory for Buck, who then becomes the lead dog. In his position of leadership, he quickly proves himself to be superior to all the other dogs and thus wins the admiration of his masters, François and Perrault, who work with Buck quite sometime before they are called away to other duties.

Buck's next master is a Scotch half-breed; the man is fair, but he works Buck almost beyond endurance, so much so that on a difficult run against extremely adverse conditions, most of the other dogs succumb to the wild elements. Buck, however, survives, even though he loses a significant amount of weight. Buck's next change in life occurs when he and his team are sold to three amateur adventurers — Charles, Hal, and Mercedes; they have absolutely no concept of how to discipline the dogs or even how to drive a team through the frozen northern snow. As a result of their ineptitude, the dogs' food supply is gone before the trip is half over. At this point, Buck sees the futility of trying to continue; thus, he simply refuses to return to the trace (the harness) despite the fact that he is severely beaten. Propitiously, a man named John Thornton appears and threatens the three owners if they continue to beat Buck.

Buck's instinct concerning the three amateur adventurers proves to be correct; Charles, Hal, and Mercedes continue on their way across the frozen snow and ice and lose their lives, plus the lives of the rest of the dog team when they try to cross a river of melting ice. All are drowned.

Meanwhile, John Thornton, who is recuperating from frost-bitten feet, nurses Buck back to health and wins from Buck a deep devotion and loyalty. Yet, even though Buck is tamed to a certain extent by the kindness of his new master, at times while he sits with John Thornton in the depths of the forest, Buck hears mysterious calls from the wild — calls which awaken long-sleeping instincts within him.

As John Thornton returns to civilization with Buck, a drunken miner attacks John Thornton and threatens to do him harm. Buck immediately reacts and kills the man. Later on, John Thornton is lost in some fast river rapids, and once again Buck saves his master's life by swimming to him with a tow line. On another occasion, Thornton makes a brag that Buck can pull a sled with a thousand pounds loaded atop it. Because of his great love for John Thornton, Buck finally succeeds in moving the heavy sled one hundred yards.

With the money that Thornton wins from his betting feat, six-teen hundred dollars, he goes deep into the wilderness in search of a fabled lost gold mine. There, he works long and hard hours, and while Thornton's men are panning for gold, Buck often goes off by himself in the wilderness in order to stalk wild animals, or catch salmon, or run with the wild wolves; one time, he even spends four days stalking a huge bull moose. Returning to camp, Buck discovers that everyone, including John Thornton, has been killed by Yeehat Indians. Without thinking and without fear, Buck attacks the entire group of Indians, killing several and driving the rest away in such fear that the valley in which Buck revenges his master is from then on considered by the Indians to be a demonic place.

After John Thornton's death, Buck is free of all his attachments to civilization, and so he joins the wild wolves, and as legend has it, he becomes the sire of a new breed of wild dogs which still exists in the wild places of the Great North, loping through the cold nights, with Buck leading them, singing "the song of the pack."

LIST OF CHARACTERS

The following human beings appear in the book:

Judge Miller

Buck's owner; a man who owns a huge plantation in California's Santa Clara Valley.

Molly and Alice Miller

The Judge's daughters whom Buck protects when they go on long walks.

Manuel

A Mexican; one of the Judge's gardener's helpers. Because of his mounting gambling debts, Manuel steals Buck and sells him to a ring of dognappers.

The Man in the Red Sweater

An unnamed person whom Buck remembers for the rest of his life because this is the person who teaches Buck the lesson that "a man with a club was a lawgiver, a master to be obeyed."

Perrault and François

Two Frenchmen who are Buck's first new masters. They work for the Canadian government, delivering dispatches to outposts throughout the frozen North.

A Scotch Half-breed

Buck's second master; he also delivers mail in the North. He is a competent master, but because of the demands made on him, he has to overwork the dogs.

"Black" Burton

A vicious man who attacks Thornton; he, in turn, is attacked by Buck.

An Ape-like Man

A "hairy" man with a bent back; he accompanies the Scotch half-breed on the mail routes.

Charles

An inept middle-aged master of Buck's; Charles comes from the South, and he does not understand the ways of the North or how to handle dogs.

Mercedes

Charles's wife; she attempts to live in the North as if she were on an "extended social camping trip."

Hal

Mercedes's brother; he carries a whip, a gun, and a knife, and he is cruel to Buck.

John Thornton

The man who rescues Buck from Charles, Hal, and Mercedes, and he is the man to whom Buck becomes immensely devoted.

Hans and Pete

John Thornton's partners; they accompany him on his expedition for the lost gold mine.

Matthewson

The man who bets Thornton that Buck cannot pull a thousand-pound loaded sled.

Jim O'Brien

John Thornton's friend; he lends Thornton a thousand dollars to make the wager with Matthewson.

The Yeehats

A fierce tribe of Indians who murder John Thornton and his partners, Hans and Pete.

The following animals play an important role in this novel and have characteristics very similar to those of human beings (called anthropomorphism):

Buck

This dog is the "main character" of the novel. Buck's father was a huge Saint Bernard, and Buck's mother was a huge Scotch shepherd dog. The central concern of *The Call of the Wild* is Buck's transformation from a civilized dog of the South to an animal capable of coping with the most adverse conditions in the Far North. Buck is used to illustrate London's idea of the "survival of the fittest" and the retreat to the potential primitive or primordial beast which lies within each animal or individual. This is also a magnification of the philosophy of naturalism, a philosophy which London was often concerned with in his writings.

Curly

Buck's friend and companion on the arduous boat trip to the North. Curly is described as a "good-natured Newfoundland." Curly does not survive long, however, and Buck learns a painful lesson when he sees how easily Curly is killed while trying to be friendly with another dog.

Spitz

The dog which kills Curly; not unexpectedly, Spitz becomes Buck's most bitter enemy. Later, Spitz is killed by Buck in a dog fight incident which is central to the novel. Buck's victory entitles him to take over the commanding power position which once belonged to Spitz. Buck's fight-to-the-death with Spitz illustrates Buck's ability to survive among even the most primitive elements.

Dave, Billee, Joe, Sol-leks, Dolly, Pike, and Dub

Other dogs which serve on the dogsled team with Buck.

Skeet and Nig

Two of John Thornton's dogs which he owned before he adopts Buck.

SUMMARIES AND COMMENTARIES

Chapter 1. Into the Primitive

The four-line poem that begins the novel summarizes the essential theme of the entire work. As noted in the section at the end of this study guide, entitled "Critical Theories," we see that London is writing in a certain literary tradition and under the influence of a literary philosophy called Naturalism. The concepts of Naturalism are summarized in these first four opening lines — that is, within every individual, however civilized, there lies deep within him a "ferine strain," which means that there is a "primitive beast" within each of us which can emerge at any particular moment, and it will emerge more quickly in periods of extreme stress. The "brumal sleep" refers to these forces that are hibernating and which will, at the proper moment, awaken and assume their bestial qualities.

In conjunction with the above ideas, London will use Buck, the enormous, extraordinarily powerful dog, as an anthropomorphic example of similar qualities for all of humankind. (*Anthropomorphic* simply means attributing human qualities to an animal.) For example, throughout the novel, Buck will be seen to possess various types of qualities that are traditionally attributed only to human beings. In one instance, we will see him possessing such qualities as loyalty, love, revenge, ambition, and other qualities usually associated with human beings. Other qualities will also be pointed out as we progress through the novel.

To emphasize his essential theme, London has the dog Buck being born on a large estate in the Southland (Santa Clara Valley, California). Buck does not know that there is a "yellow metal" recently discovered in the Far North and that strong, powerful dogs are desperately needed and will bring a rather large price. While Buck is a very large dog – his father was a huge Saint Bernard and his mother was a Scotch shepherd – Buck has lived a comfortable life of ease in very civilized surroundings. London writes that Buck "had lived the life of a sated aristocrat." Buck's master was the gentle and kind Judge Miller, the epitome of a highly civilized society. The fact that London chooses the Judge for Buck's master strongly underscores the fact that we are to be aware of civilization's laws, its customs, and all of the machinations of order.

Having established Buck, then, as a product of civilization, London will, as his chapter title "Into the Primitive" indicates, now show the contrast between Buck, the civilized dog, and the dog he becomes when he is suddenly thrust into a life completely different. This comes about because one of Judge Miller's servants, Manuel, has amassed significant gambling debts and in order to repay the debts, Manuel sells Buck to some traders dealing in dognapping. These dogs will later be sold to gold prospectors in the North. We must always remember the contrast that London is utilizing in this novel: Buck comes not only from civilization, but also from a life of unusual ease and comfort, where all of his food is provided for him; he is *not* accustomed to killing in order to eat. In fact, "over this great demesne [Judge Miller's estate] Buck ruled." Later in the North, Buck will also rule, in effect, as the "king" of the dogsled group, but he will have to fight – literally fight for his life – in order to have the right to rule over the other dogs.

Buck's gigantic size makes him a special prize for the dognappers. While Manuel receives only $50.00 for his part of the transaction, Buck will later bring a price of $300.00, and later on, he will bring even larger sums. In Chapter 6, for instance, $1200.00 will be offered as a buying price for Buck.

At present, however, Buck is a trusting dog, and he has no idea what fate holds for him; therefore, he has no inkling of Manuel's treachery: "he had learned to trust in men he knew, and to give them credit for a wisdom that outreached his own." But now that Buck is tied by the throat by strangers and is treated violently, he becomes enraged, and in his "unbridled anger," he closes his jaws on the hand of the man who is holding him, and Buck does not let go until he is tied around the throat so tightly that his senses are choked out of him and he collapses.

Eventually, Buck regains consciousness, but every time he resists his tormenters, he is thrown down and choked repeatedly. He is totally confused by the meaning of such brutality from these strange men and is "oppressed by the vague sense of impending calamity."

As the men gradually proceed to file off Judge Miller's heavy brass collar from Buck's neck, we realize that these men are filing off the last vestige of civilization. Afterward, Buck is thrown into a cage. It is ironic that in civilization, Buck was free to roam, but now, taken from his familiar surroundings, he is brutally flung into a cage. Buck's reaction is to become more and more ferocious, as he attempts time and again, unsuccessfully, to break out of the bars. For two days and two nights, Buck neither eats nor drinks; his eyes become bloodshot and, finally, he is "metamorphosed into a raging fiend." By the time that the train carrying Buck reaches Seattle, he is so changed, says London, that not even Judge Miller would recognize him.

At Seattle, Buck is delivered into the hands of a "stout man with a red sweater and a club." To this man, Buck seems to be hardly a dog; the man calls Buck a "truly red-eyed devil," and again and again, Buck attempts to attack the man in the red sweater; as a result, Buck is taught the first law of primitive society – that is, a man with a club in his hand is more powerful than a single dog. London refers to this "lesson" as the "law of the club." Significantly, the man in the red sweater finally admits that Buck is indeed a powerful and great adversary. Once Buck has learned that the "law of the club" is a law that he must obey, he allows the man in the red sweater to bring him water to drink and food to eat; he even eats the food from the man's hand. It is obvious that Buck knows that he is beaten, but, as London tells us, Buck is *not* broken: he was beaten (he knew that), "but he was not broken." To Buck, the man with the club, a kind of "cave man" figure, represents the potential for the primitive element in all of us. The red of his sweater hearkens us to recall Buck's blood-red eyes and also the blood which Buck is covered with after his beating, as well as the red blood of raw meat. *Red*, therefore, serves as a symbol of savagery.

Even though Buck recognizes that a man with a club is a master to be obeyed, yet Buck does not do what some dogs do – that is, he does not fawn upon the man-master, but then neither does Buck struggle for mastery for so long that he is killed in the struggle – as some dogs actually do. Buck is *always* able to judge just how far to resist before giving up. This is how he learns to deal with the man in the red sweater, and throughout the rest of the novel, Buck will always remember the man with the red sweater, for this is his introduction to the "law of the club" and to the laws of the primitive world.

Buck is next sold to a man named Perrault, a Frenchman, who recognizes Buck as "one in ten thousand," as he puts it. In fact, Perrault buys two dogs – Buck (for $300.00) and another dog, Curly, a "good-natured Newfoundland." Perrault then takes both dogs aboard a ship, the *Narwhal*, where Buck encounters Perrault's partner, François. Buck "speedily learned that Perrault and François were fair men, calm and impartial in administering justice" and, most important, "too wise in the ways of dogs to be fooled by dogs." Throughout the novel, Buck will *constantly* evaluate his human owners in terms of their competence. Furthermore, he will never resent hard work – if it is administered with impartiality.

Buck soon discovers that there are other dogs below deck, and after an indeterminate length of time, they all dock in a northern port, and there Buck encounters something entirely new: he discovers "white stuff that was falling through the air." This is his first encounter with snow. At first, it puzzles him, but when some on-lookers laugh at him, he feels ashamed. Here is another example of London's use of anthropomorphism: Buck is endowed with the human qualities of shame and embarrassment. Furthermore, the snow represents Buck's first encounter with an element of nature which he will have to contend with for the rest of his life.

In general, then, this chapter has taken Buck from the ease and comfort of civilization through his first encounter with the law of the primitive, when he was being beaten with a club, to his arrival somewhere in the Far North, and his true geographical entry into "the primitive."

Chapter 2. The Law of Club and Fang

This chapter will introduce London's second, or parallel, theme of the novel. As a matter of historical and scientific information, the late nineteenth century had seen the emergence of Charles Darwin's theory of evolution, a theory which had become, by the time of London's novel, one of the most controversial scientific theories ever advocated. In a nutshell, the essence of Darwin's theory concerns the evolution of mankind – that is, was Man born as he is today? Or is he the end result of a series of evolutions from a more primitive species of life? In other words, in a more popular conception, is Man descended from apelike creatures? This theory, then, is further emphasized by London's use of the "survival of the fittest" (which also carries the opposite connotation of the elimination of the weakest). This chapter introduces Buck into the concepts of the survival of the fittest, and we will see how Buck is able to confront new and different situations, and how he is able to maintain his mastery of life – even in the most adverse conditions. In fact, at the very beginning of the chapter, London emphasizes this contrast: during Buck's first day, London tells us, "every hour was filled with shock and surprise. Buck had been suddenly jerked from the heart of civilization and flung into the heart of things primordial. No lazy, sun-kissed life was this, with nothing to do but loaf and be bored." In fact, Buck learned the law of the club rapidly in the previous chapter; now he will learn the "law of the fang." London is emphasizing that the respected laws of civilization have to be discarded if a man or a beast is to survive in this primitive situation. Buck learns immediately that he must be "constantly alert, for these dogs and men were not town dogs and men; they were savages." In this new society, Buck intuitively recognizes that only the strongest will survive. This is illustrated by the death of the good-natured dog called Curly, who, once he is wounded and down, is surrounded by thirty or forty other dogs, anxiously waiting to close in upon Curly, waiting for the primitive kill. What Buck witnesses is so unexpected and horrible that he is stunned by the entire episode, and, in fact, as he sees Curly's limp and lifeless body lying in the bloodied snow, he realizes that there is "no fair play" in this world, and that "once down, that was the end of you." In Buck's later life, he will often remember this gory, unjust scene; it will "trouble his sleep" many times. (We can thus anticipate that Buck's memory of this scene will cause him to hold his ground in later dog fights and to be savagely alert and bold.)

When Buck is harnessed to a sled by Francois, he is placed between Spitz, the lead dog, and Dave, "an experienced wheeler." (A "wheeler" is the dog nearest the sled.) At first, Buck resents being placed in a harness, as though he were merely some "draft animal" that he remembers from civilization, but Buck is too wise to rebel against this treatment, because he knows that François is "stern in demanding obedience, and Buck [knows] that he would not hesitate to use the whip." For the code of the Far North, the whip is tantamount to what the club was in Buck's first lesson concerning the "law of the club." Buck learns his duties very quickly, and one of the important laws of the primitive world is that one *must* learn quickly if one is to adapt to new situations and survive. For example, after his first day as a sled dog, Buck learns to "stop at 'ho,' and to go ahead at 'mush.' "

Buck's next learning experience involves the three new dogs that Perrault acquires. Two of these dogs, Billee and Joe, are huskies and brothers, but they are quite different in temperament. The third dog, however, Sol-leks (meaning "the angry one"), is blind in one eye, and he does not like to be approached on his blind side. Once, when Buck forgetfully approaches Sol-leks from the blind side, Sol-leks hurls himself upon Buck and slashes Buck's shoulder to the bone. Forever afterward, Buck avoids Sol-lek's blind side. Thus, continually, Buck learns an entirely new way of living and existing. Yet he and Sol-leks are not enemies because of the episode mentioned above, and until the death of Sol-leks, he and Buck are good friends.

Buck's next lesson in adapting to his new life involves finding a warm place to sleep. He sees lights one night in François and Perrault's tent, and because he has been used to sleeping by the Judge's fireplace, Buck enters their tent, only to be bombarded by curses and flying objects. Wandering around the camp site in the cold bitter wind, which is penetrating his wounded shoulder, Buck is surprised to find that all of the other dogs are, as it were, "teammates," and that they have buried themselves under the snow. Thus, Buck learns how the other dogs sleep and keep warm, so he selects a place for himself and is soon asleep; once again, he learns another lesson about how to survive in this new and hostile country.

Next morning, when Buck awakens, he feels the weight of the night's snow pressing down upon him, and "a great surge of fear swept through him – the fear of the wild thing for the trap." London, quite pointedly, goes on to say that this fear was "a token that [Buck] was harking back through his own life to the lives of his forebears." London writes, "the muscles of [Buck's] whole body contracted spasmodically and instinctively," and bursting out through the layer of snow, he sees the camp spread out before him. That day, Buck has another experience learning to be a sled dog, similar to the incident referred to earlier in these Notes. Buck is now placed between Dave and Sol-leks, who are both experienced dogs and who will teach Buck how to perform. When Buck makes a mistake, both dogs instantly "administer a sound trouncing to him." Buck learns very quickly, and at the end of that day, he is exhausted; after digging his hole in the snow, he falls quickly asleep.

For days, Buck is constantly "in the traces," and even though he is given a half pound of food a day more than the other dogs, he never seems to have enough, and he suffers from perpetual hunger pains. This is due partly to the fact that Buck is a civilized dog and a fastidious eater, and the other dogs wolf down their food, then come over and steal Buck's rations. Buck quickly learns, however, that in order to survive, he too must wolf down his food. In a civilized society, Buck would never have had to steal food, but now he realizes that in order to survive and thrive in this hostile northern environment, he will have to learn to steal in very secret and clever ways. According to London, Buck's thefts of food "marked the decay or going to pieces of his moral nature." But what Buck is learning is that in such a wilderness as this, his old sense of morality is a hindrance to survival.

Buck, however, reasons that in order to survive, he *must* adjust — in every way he can. It was one thing to respect private property in the Southland, where the law of love and fellowship reigned, but here in the Northland, "under the law of club and fang, it was foolhardy to observe any law that did not contribute to one's own personal survival." London writes that, although Buck did not exactly figure this out in "thoughts," the man in the red sweater had taught him about this very fundamental and primitive code. Buck's "decivilization was now almost complete because he did not steal out of joy," and "he did not rob openly, but, instead, he stole secretly and cunningly out of respect for club and fang."

Continuing with this concept of the survival of the fittest, Buck also soon learns that he can eat any type of food (even loathsome food) so long as doing so will help him survive. Furthermore, Buck's sight, his scent, and his hearing quickly develop a keenness which he never knew in civilized society. He is now even able to scent the wind, and he can tell what the weather will be like a night in advance. "And not only did he learn by experience, but instincts long dead had become alive again."

Carrying through with London's concept of naturalism (which maintains that there is a dimension of the primitive in all of us), Buck is beginning to remember back to ancient times before his own existence, to a time "when wild dogs ranged in packs through the primeval forest and killed their meat as they ran it down." Furthermore, on cold nights, Buck often points his nose toward the sky and howls like a wolf; "it was as though his ancestors . . . [were] pointing their noses at the stars and howling down the centuries and through him." This anticipates the final chapter of the novel when Buck will be seen roaming the forest with the wolf pack and will be seen answering the call of the wild by howling with the other wolves.

Chapter 3. The Dominant Primordial Beast

London begins this chapter by stating that the "dominant primordial beast was strong in Buck," meaning that the primitive will to survive was now *the primary factor* in Buck's life. Thus, the entire chapter is constructed to show Buck's will and determination to survive. Buck's survival instinct will be climaxed at the end of this chapter in a dramatic fight-to-the-death scene between Buck and his archrival, Spitz. Just as the chapter begins with an emphasis on "the dominant primordial beast," it ends with the same words, emphasizing the central concern of the chapter: the survival of the fittest.

At the beginning of the chapter, Buck has been avoiding fights whenever possible, but there still exists a bitter hatred between him and Spitz, and if we review Chapter 1, where Buck had his first encounter with the Spitzbergen (Spitz, in shortened form), we will remember that Spitz is the dog that first stole Buck's food. Furthermore, at the beginning of Chapter 2, Spitz is the dog who watched with pleasure when Curly was killed. And now, in this chapter, Spitz is the leader of the dogsled team, which arouses Buck's jealousy. Buck was accustomed to being the head dog at Judge Miller's estate, and now he has to take a subordinate position, and it is insulting to his pride. An ultimate confrontation between Buck and Spitz seems inevitable, and in this chapter, we are first given a short, but vicious encounter between Buck and Spitz, when Buck returns to his nest to find Spitz occupying his sleeping hole. This arouses the "beast" in Buck, and he springs upon Spitz "with a fury which surprised them both." There probably would have been a fearful, bloody fight at that time if it had not been for Francois and Perrault, who quickly surmise the situation and put an end to the fight. At the same time, however, the fight between the two dogs is delayed by the sudden appearance of "four or five score of starving huskies" who invade the camp. These starving huskies ignore the clubs which flail them, and they attempt to consume all of the food supplies.

In the meantime, the sled dogs have burst from their nests in order to protect their food. Then, however, all of the team dogs are attacked by the wild dogs and even the team dogs revert to primitive behavior. London tells us that they "fought the wild dogs with a fierceness." Buck is especially excited by the taste of blood after he sinks his teeth into one of the wild dogs. The taste of blood goads him to "greater fierceness." The sled team dogs eventually escape to the wilderness, but are seriously wounded. Some lose an eye, some lose an ear, and all have gaping wounds; eventually, though, they return to the camp site and find that François and Perrault have driven the wild dogs away. Half of the food supply, however, is gone. This key incident shows the wild, untamed fury of the starving animals who contain a fury which indicates the instinctual desire for survival. Furthermore, in the encounter with the wild huskies, Spitz, rather than fight against a common enemy, uses the opportunity to attack Buck – on two different occasions. The first time occurs when Buck is fighting a wild huskie, and Spitz viciously attacks him from the side; the second time occurs when Spitz rushes upon Buck in an attempt to throw Buck in the path of the wild huskies, an event which Buck realizes would have meant certain death. There have now been three encounters between Buck, the dog of the Southland, and Spitz, the opportunistic dog of the Northland.

With the food supplies half gone, and with four hundred miles of wild trail ahead, François and Perrault begin to lead the dogs on a dangerous journey. It takes the sled team six days to cross the thirty miles that make up the "Thirty Mile River" because the ice keeps breaking under them, and they have to stop and build fires to dry out or else they will freeze to death. At one time, the ice breaks and Spitz, the lead dog, falls in, dragging the entire team, except Buck, in with him. During the rescue, which requires most of the day, another day of travel is lost.

Being a dog from civilization, Buck's paws are not accustomed to the harshness of the trail, and François often has to bring Buck's food rations to him; finally, he makes a pair of moccasins which will fit over Buck's paws. They are a great relief to the dog. One morning, a surprising event occurs. The dog Dolly, a particularly mild-mannered dog, suddenly begins "a long, heartbreaking wolf howl," which indicates that she has suddenly gone mad. Frothing at the mouth and snarling, Dolly begins to chase Buck, who flees in confused terror from her. After plunging through the woods and through ice, with Dolly snarling only one leap behind him, Buck finally passes through the camp site, where François holds an ax, poised in his hand. Thus he does what he must: he smashes the ax down on the mad dog's head.

The incident is exhausting, and Buck staggers along the trail, completely worn out. The nasty tempered Spitz takes Buck's weakened condition as an opportunity to attack him once more, and twice he tears Buck's flesh to the bone. François, however, is close by, and using the whip, he beats Spitz away. But Buck can no longer forgive Spitz, and from this moment on, it is all-out war between Spitz and Buck. Buck constantly challenges Spitz's authority and uses every chance he can to undermine Spitz's authority. London writes that it was "inevitable that the fight for leadership should come." Buck's pride is such that he does not like to be subservient to any dog – most of all to Spitz.

All the way to Dawson, there is continual bickering between Buck and Spitz, and this conflict is important, of course, because ideally a dog team must work as a single unit, and when a dog mutinies, that dog ceases to be effective. More important, though, is London's focus on the struggle between the civilized dog from the South and the primitive dog from the North. London's point here is that the cunningness that Buck learned in civilization combined with his superior strength and his newly acquired primeval instincts make Buck the superior animal in what will be a coming, critical contest between him and Spitz.

After seven days in Dawson, during which time the dogs recuperate, they begin the return trip. It is imperative, however, that they cover the distance as rapidly as possible, but this is partly facilitated by the fact that they are going to travel light, and that the mounted police have deposited supplies along the way, plus the fact that the trail which they have already broken will be easier to travel. In spite of these added conveniences, though, the trip is slowed by the dissension between Buck and Spitz, and this is due, in large part, to the fact that Buck has undermined the authority of Spitz, and this has caused the other dogs to rebel. It is now even more obvious that the inevitable fight between Buck and Spitz will take place – and soon.

This climactic fight occurs when one of the dogs, Dub, startles a snowshoe rabbit. As the rabbit attempts to escape, all of the other dogs join in the chase. The chase greatly excites Buck's primitive, ecstatic instincts – "the blood lust, the joy to kill"; he is impassioned to kill with his teeth and savor the fresh, warm blood. Spitz, however, while Buck is enjoying the chase, becomes cold and calculating; he cuts across a narrow neck of land and captures the rabbit. Buck is furious and is so frenzied by the wild desire for fresh blood, as well as so fiercely enraged over Spitz's actions, that he realizes that the time has finally come – that the time for the critical battle between him and Spitz has arrived.

Spitz is the more experienced fighter and is able to ward off most of Buck's charges. In fact, Buck almost exhausts himself in his repeated, vicious attacks, as Spitz slashes Buck's shoulder; Spitz is, for awhile, seemingly the superior dog. But just as Buck reaches the point of exhaustion, he uses that "quality that made for greatness – imagination." Previously, Buck was fighting by instinct, but now he chooses to fight by imagination and intellect. He pretends to make one more halfhearted dash at Spitz's throat, but, instead, he quickly reverses himself and crunches down on Spitz's left foreleg, breaking it. After successive tries, repeating the same gesture, Buck is able to break Spitz's other foreleg. By now, Spitz is down, and the other dogs begin circling around them, waiting for the kill. In London's words, "Buck was inexorable. Mercy was a thing reserved for gentler climes." Thus, the bestial instinct has been proven in Buck's superiority to Spitz, and after he has defeated Spitz, we see that Buck, a previously highly civilized dog from the South, has now defeated the strong, brave, uncivilized dog from the North. Buck has become, without question, "the dominant primordial beast."

Chapter 4. Who Has Won to Mastership

The next day, Francois and Perrault discover that Spitz is missing, and the signs of battle on Buck's body are proof that the inevitable battle between Buck and Spitz has occurred, and that Buck is the obvious winner. François is pleased because he knows that now there will be no more trouble with the dogs working as a team. A major decision must be made, however. Since Spitz has been killed, the sled drivers require a new lead dog. Sol-leks is chosen as the new lead dog. But Buck will not allow this, and he springs upon Sol-leks in a fury, indicating his desire to be the leader of the pack. François separates the dogs several times, but his tries are futile because Buck attacks Sol-leks again and again. Finally, François gets a club and threatens Buck with it. Buck immediately remembers the man in the red sweater, and he cowers before the club. Yet "Buck was in open revolt," and he springs upon Sol-leks at the first opportunity.

Perrault and François chase Buck around the camp site for about an hour, but Buck easily eludes them. Then realizing that they are losing precious time, the drivers finally yield to Buck's wishes and install him as the lead dog. Buck more than proves his prowess. Immediately, he "shows himself" the superior even of Spitz, of whom François had never seen the equal.

Buck continues to excel in leadership, and the other dogs fall immediately in line and grant Buck his hard-earned superiority. In fact, one of the dogs, Pike, lagging during the day, is soundly punished by Buck for his laziness. Thus the team begins operating in its old superior form, a fact which pleases François and Perrault very much. At one of the stops, the Rink Rapids, two native huskies, Teek and Koona, are added to the team, and Buck immediately coerces them into being members of the team. In record time, the journey from the Rink Rapids to Skagway, their destination, is accomplished.

For three days, Perrault and François brag about their accomplishments, and "the team [is] the constant center of a worshipful crowd of dog busters and mushers." New orders, however, come to the kindly drivers, François and Perrault, and "like other men, they are forced to accept new assignments, and so they leave Buck's life. Buck's new owner is a "Scotch half-breed" and is known only by that name; he is the driver of the mail team over the trail to Dawson. Once again, Buck and his mates set out on the weary and monotonous trail to Dawson. We are told that Buck enjoyed lying near the campfire, at which time he would dream of his old life in the Santa Clara Valley, but – and this is an important point – "he was not homesick." The Sunland was very "dim and distant," and such old memories have no power over him any more. At other times, he ponders the "half-breed cook" who also sits near the campfire. In London's description of the "half-breed cook," it is clear that he wants us to see the half-breed as a type of prehistoric cave man covered with hair, a creature perhaps closer to the animals than to the humans. We are told that "he did not stand erect," but that he had "a trunk that inclined forward from the hips on legs bent at the knees." He is described as a "hairy man" who slept with his "head between his legs."

Buck and his mates are in poor condition due to the lack of rest and recuperation at Skagway, and to make matters worse is the fact that on the way to Dawson, it snows every day, making the journey even more tedious. Once again, London reminds us of his central concern about the survival of the fittest. He tells us that since Buck's career as a sled dog began, he has traveled over 1800 miles, and that 1800 miles will take its toll—even on "the life of the toughest."

One day, Dave, one of the sled dogs, becomes irritable and constantly cries out in intense pain. The drivers can locate no broken bones or visible wounds, but they know that something is wrong, probably internally. The Scotch half-breed, therefore, decides to remove Dave from the team; yet Dave, even in his pain, is resentful. London explains that "the pride of trace and trail was his, and, sick unto death, he could not bear that another dog should do his work." So he runs alongside the sled, which causes him excruciating pain because he deeply desires to be a member of the team. The driver is concerned by Dave's actions, and his comrades "talked of how a dog could break its heart through being denied the work that killed it." The driver decides to harness Dave again, even though he knows that it will surely kill him. The next morning, Dave is too weak to travel, but through an incredible act of physical stamina, Dave bravely stands in line to be harnessed. He constantly trips and falls, and he stumbles, unable to pull along with his teammates, and at last, the driver is forced to remove Dave from the team. Retracing his steps to the camp, the Scotch half-breed takes Dave back with him, and as Buck listens from a distance, there is a crack of a revolver, ending Dave's life on the trail.

In general, this chapter functions as something very much like a transitional chapter. In the first three chapters, we saw how Buck adjusted to the primitive wilderness and to the primeval North. After his winning his mastership in this chapter, we see that Buck now performs the tests of his masters with perfect precision, making himself a lead dog superior even to all the other dogs. Thus, Buck proves to be a perfect creature. This transitional chapter contrasts with the first three chapters, then, and the next three chapters will show Buck becoming increasingly alien to all traces of civilization and preparing himself to accept and adapt to "the call of the wild."

Chapter 5. The Toil of Trace and Trail

This chapter begins thirty days after the dogs have made the long pull back to Skagway, after having successfully delivered the mail to Dawson. By now, Buck has lost over thirty-five pounds, and he is not alone in his suffering; in fact, all of the dogs are in a wretched state. They are all overworked, they have sore paws, they are plagued with injuries, and, in general, they are exhausted – dead tired. Furthermore, there is "no power of recuperation left, no reserve strength to call upon. In this chapter, we discover that in the last five months they have traveled twenty-five thousand miles with only five days' rest.

The drivers expect a long recuperation period, but because of the droves of people who have arrived in the great North, the mail is arriving at a rapid pace, necessitating constant mail runs. Worthless or tired and weak dogs, London tells us, are "gotten rid of." Thus, before the team is fully rested, two men from the States buy them – "harness and all, for a song" – meaning that they were bought very cheaply. The two men are Hal and Charles. Charles, the older, is middle-aged with watery eyes and a fiercely uptwisted light mustache. Hal is younger, probably nineteen or twenty, and he carries a gun and a hunting knife – a detail which London includes to emphasize Hal's callousness and his potential evil. The two men are accompanied by Mercedes, who is Charles's wife and Hal's sister. London never tells the reader exactly why these people have come to the great North; instead, they seem to be here only to illustrate another aspect of the type of life that Buck has had to become accustomed to if he is to adjust to all aspects of this new and primitive existence. Until this event, Buck's masters have all known critical ways of coping with the North – that is, they know how to drive, how to survive, and how to treat the team. Now, however, Buck is confronted with inept people who cannot cope with the violence of the wilderness and the great North. Consequently, we will now see how Buck responds and adjusts to human ineptitude.

The first example of Buck's new masters' ineptitude is the tent, which is awkwardly assembled. In addition, the dishes are packed unwashed, and no one has any concept as to how to load and pack the sled. Furthermore, when the three attempt to leave, the dogs are unable to budge the sled; ignorantly, Hal assumes that this is merely incompetence on the part of the dogs, and he beats them severely, lashing them viciously with his whip. A man from a neighboring tent attempts to defend the dogs, claiming that "they are plumb tuckered out," and another incensed onlooker tells the three that the sled runners are frozen fast in the snow; this is the reason why the dogs cannot budge the sled. Here again is more proof of the trio's ineptitude — and what is far worse is their basic ignorance of the techniques of dealing with the conditions of the great North. Throughout the beatings of the dogs, Mercedes objects strongly, but at the same time, she is resentful of the fact that some of the things which she has packed must be tossed off the sled. During the course of this trip, we will discover why Mercedes changes as drastically as she does; eventually, however, her present concern for the dogs will be replaced by a concern for only herself.

The sled's runners are finally freed from the frozen snow, but the dogs still have to struggle with all their might in order to pull the sled even a short distance, and when the path becomes uneven, the sled overturns and spills most of the load, which, as we know, has been improperly loaded. Once the dogs are freed from the excess weight, they flee without heeding the calls of their "new masters." Buck and his comrades look upon these people with a great deal of suspicion.

Later, when Mercedes refuses to cast away as much of her possessions as the onlookers advocated, Charles and Hal decide to buy six extra dogs, now making a total of fourteen dogs pulling the sled. The extra dogs, of course, require more food proportionately, and this increases the load which the dogs must pull. As the days go by, London says, it becomes apparent, even to Buck, that "they were slack in all things, without order or discipline."

For example, it takes them an unduly long time to pitch the camp at nighttime, and the morning is always well underway before they are able to break camp. This delay not only is cutting into the distance which they need to cover each day, but it is also eating into the food supply that is supposed to last them throughout the trip. Added to these difficulties is the fact that Mercedes steals extra food and gives it to the dogs on the sly. This is also complicated by the fact that when the dogs do not pull the sled fast enough, Hal beats them severely, further sapping their strength. Arguments among the three people occur constantly; not only "did they not know how to work the dogs, they did not know how to work themselves." When Hal, taking stock of the food supply, discovers that the food is half gone and that they have traversed only one-fourth of the way, he cuts down on the dogs' rations so badly that it weakens all of the dogs, especially the new dogs, who are not accustomed to the severities of the dogsled and the elements.

By this time, Hal, Charles, and Mercedes are too irritable and miserable to even quarrel with one another. In addition, the dogs begin dying off one by one, until only five experienced dogs remain. Apparently, no one seems to be concerned, for in the dissension among the three people, all consideration for the dogs has faded away and even though Mercedes weighs only one hundred and twenty pounds, she demands to ride on the sled, which increases the burden of the already weakened, starving, and suffering dogs.

At a place called "the Five Fingers," the dog food gives out completely, but the men are able to trade a revolver for some frozen, dried horsehide, which the dogs find irritating and indigestible.

Hal continues to beat the dogs, and those that are left can hardly pull the sled, especially with the additional weight of Mercedes on it. The fierce winter has now given away to spring, but there is no food, and as the last reserve strength of the dogs fades, they arrive at John Thornton's camp.

Thornton is an experienced man of the North, and he immediately perceives that Hal has achieved all of his boastful tasks only by one ploy – by severely punishing the dogs. Thus, when it is time to leave Thornton's camp, Buck, who has always been able to somehow summon an extra measure of strength, simply refuses to move. Instinctively, he knows that with the coming of spring that these inept new "masters" do not know how to cope with the dangers that the melting snow and ice will present. London says: "It seemed that Buck sensed disaster close at hand, out there ahead on the ice." Therefore, despite the tremendous blows administered by Hal, Buck refuses to move, and, ultimately, John Thornton, "convulsed with rage" at Hal's merciless stupidity, steps between Hal and Buck, and he threatens Hal's life if he strikes Buck again. Hitting Hal's knuckles with his ax handle, Thornton knocks Hal's knife loose and uses it to cut Buck loose from his harness. Meanwhile, Hal and Charles are too busy with Mercedes to retaliate against Thornton, and, before long, Buck raises his head just in time to see the other four dogs – Pike, Solleks, Joe, and Teek – limping and staggering across the thawing ice. As Buck and Thornton watch, they see a yawning hole in the middle of a patch of ice, and then a whole section of the ice gives way, and all of them – dogs and humans – disappear.

In this chapter, London shows three inexperienced people from the Southland, confronted by entirely different circumstances in the great North, and he shows their inability to adjust to such extremely diverse circumstances. Each of the three, Mercedes especially, tries to bring too much of "civilization" with them into this extremely uncivilized country. London has nothing but contempt for these inept wanderers of the North, who have no business being there. In contrast, John Thornton has a great deal of compassion for the dogs who pull the sled, but even he shows very little compassion for these ignorant people of the South. Even Buck knows, by instinct, that the ice will not hold up, yet these people of so-called civilized intelligence will not – and seemingly cannot – learn how to survive in the harsh North. In other words, as London has constantly suggested, Buck's primitive instincts have taught him the means of survival against overwhelming odds, whereas these three humans succumb to the harsh vicissitudes of the Northland. Hal, Charles, and Mercedes are destroyed, finally, by their own stupidity.

Chapter 6. For the Love of a Man

In this chapter, Buck will be characterized as an animal of great love, loyalty, and devotion; he will become completely devoted to John Thornton, who is, in contrast to Hal and Charles, Buck's other masters, characterized as being the ideal "master." Not since Buck's days with Judge Miller has Buck experienced "love, genuine passionate love." Even in the Santa Clara Valley, with the Judge's son, Buck's relationship had been one of a "working partnership" and as a sort of "pompous guardianship," and even his relationship with the

Judge had been a "stately and dignified friendship." However, London now writes that the love which Buck feels for John Thornton has quickly developed into a feverish and burning admiration. Furthermore, in contrast to the events in the last chapter, where dog and man could not work together at all, here in Chapter 6, we are shown the great heights to which a dog can rise if he is inspired by love and admiration for his master. Certainly at the beginning of this chapter, he is as close to death as is physically possible, and, accordingly, Thornton devotes considerable time and patience while he is nursing Buck back to health.

As this chapter begins, we learn a bit of the history about John Thornton and how he came to be camped next to the river. The previous winter, Thornton had frozen his feet, and his partners had left him behind to recover. During both Buck's and Thornton's recoveries, there are two other of Thornton's dogs, Skeet and Nig, who are very friendly towards Buck, who is surprised; he expected them to show some signs of jealousy. Yet, unlike the other two dogs, Buck does not force Thornton's attention upon him; Buck is content to lie at a distance, watching Thornton with love and admiration. In fact, for a long time after Thornton rescues Buck, Buck is uncomfortable when Thornton is out of his sight, because Buck remembers how people like Perrault and François, and even the Scotch half-breed – all good masters – had, one day, suddenly disappeared, leaving Buck finally at the mercy of Hal, Charles, and Mercedes.

London, however, does not suddenly make Buck into an all-good, ideal, one-dimensional dog. He says that in spite of the great love which Buck has for John Thornton, Buck still retains a strong sense of the primitive. In other words, Buck's faithfulness and devotion – qualities associated with a civilized society – are apparent in his conduct toward John Thornton, but Buck still retains his protective instincts for the wild and his mastery of the primitive.

London also reminds us that Buck's body is scarred, "scored by the teeth of many dogs," so much so that other dogs would quickly acknowledge his supremacy in a fight. Buck had indeed "learned well the law of club and fang . . . he must master . . . because to show mercy was a weakness. Mercy did not exist in the primordial life . . . kill or be killed, eat or be eaten was the law." During these times, Buck relishes living with John Thornton, yet there are other, deeper claims to him also. From far deep down in the forest, he often hears wild sounds and calls that are mysteriously thrilling and com-pelling. He often ponders the nature of these mysterious calls, and he often thinks of running toward them, except for the fact that "the love of John Thornton drew him back to the fire again." When Thorn-ton's partners, Hans and Pete, arrive with the long-awaited raft, Buck refuses to acknowledge them, except as friends of Thornton. He feels loyalty only to Thornton.

At this point, London shifts his point of view from Buck to the character of John Thornton, and we discover that during their dual recuperation, Thornton develops a great admiration for Buck. One day, therefore, after Hans and Pete's arrival, Thornton and his friends are sitting on the edge of a chasm, into which Thornton sud-denly orders Buck to jump. Evidently, Thornton does this in order to demonstrate to Hans and Pete that Buck is totally devoted to him. In London's words, "The next instant he [Thorton] was grappling with Buck on the extreme edge. . . ."

Later on, in Circle City, Buck has yet another opportunity to demonstrate his devotion to John Thornton. An evil-tempered and malicious man named "Black" Burton is bullying a young "tenderfoot" in a bar (a tenderfoot is an inexperienced person in the frontier). When John Thornton tries to prevent a nasty fight, Burton strikes Thornton solidly and sends him sprawling. Immediately, Buck at-tacks the man, and even though Burton is able to protect himself from two different lunges by the dog, Buck is finally able to tear open the man's throat. A meeting is immediately called, and it is decided that Buck had sufficient provocation for defending his master against violence. Later on that year, Buck again proves his worth by again saving Thornton's life. While attempting to maneuver some dangerous rapids, Thornton's boat overturns, flinging him into the cold, swirling water, which, in turn, sweeps him into the midst of such wild rapids that not even a strong swimmer could survive. Buck does not hesitate to act; he swims out to Thornton, who knows that they are not strong enough to conquer the turbulent rapids. Thus he orders Buck back to the shore, and even though Buck hates to desert his master, he nevertheless obeys Thornton's commands. Once on shore, Hans and Pete tie a long rope to Buck's collar and send him back into the water with it. Buck launches boldly out into the stream, but finds that he cannot travel straight enough, and he misses Thorn-ton by only a few yards. Again, he returns to shore, where the rope is once again attached to him. "He had miscalculated once, but he would not be guilty of it a second time." This time, he reaches Thornton, who is able to grab the rope, and almost "strangling and suffocating," the man and the dog, both bruised and battered, are dragged back to the shore. There, they discover that Buck has two broken ribs, and Thornton announces that they will not break camp until Buck's ribs are fully healed.

A third episode concerning Buck's extraordinary character occurs sometime later, and it is such a feat that Buck's fame spreads throughout all Alaska. It begins in a saloon, where some men are boasting of the exploits of their dogs. Thornton is intrigued and is driven to maintain that Buck can pull a sled with a thousand pounds on it. Furthermore, he says, Buck can break the sled loose – even if it is frozen fast – and, furthermore, that he can pull it a hundred yards. A man named Matthewson bets Thornton that Buck cannot do such an incredible feat; in fact, he is willing to bet a thousand dollars that Buck cannot do it. Thornton, at this point, momentarily becomes unsure whether or not Buck can actually perform such an enormous and appalling task, and he is confused as to what to do, since neither he, nor Hans, nor Pete has a thousand dollars. At that moment, however, an old friend of Thornton's, Jim O'Brien, walks into the saloon and offers to lend Thornton a thousand dollars. The bet is on, and all of the occupants of the town pour into the streets, the men all placing great odds that Buck cannot budge the sled. When it is discovered that the sled's runners are, in fact, frozen to the ice, and Thornton is not able to break the sled loose, the odds soar tremendously. Matthewson, however, offers to increase his wager by another thousand – at three to one odds – but Thornton, Hans and Pete are able to raise only two hundred dollars, which they bet against Matthewson's six hundred.

As the contest is about to begin, John Thornton kneels beside Buck's head, whispering quiet statements of endearment: "As you love me, Buck. As you love me." Buck answers this plea by taking "his master's mittened hands between his jaws, pressing in with his teeth . . . it was the answer, in terms, not of speech, but of love." Thornton orders the dog to "MUSH," and so Buck, mustering every last bit of strength he has, every muscle and sinew straining under the tremendous weight, heaves forward. But one of Buck's feet slips, and he suddenly falls down in the snow. Yet, because of his amazing resiliency, he stands up and pulls even harder, and finally he is able to move the sled – inch by inch, foot by foot – until he finally covers the hundred yards previously marked off as being the finish line. The crowd cheers, and in appreciation, Thornton kneels by the dog. The famed "King of Skookum Bench" offers to pay Thornton a thousand dollars for Buck, but Thornton rejects the offer.

Here in this chapter, then, just before Buck will return to the primitive world, London shows us the love, the devotion, the affection, and the cooperation that can exist between a man and a dog. Under certain circumstances, especially after a man has saved a dog's life, the dog can be expected to save his master's reputation.

Chapter 7. The Sounding of the Call

So far, this novel has depicted Buck's complete transformation from the Southland civilized dog, living in the peaceful society of Judge Miller's estate in Chapter 1 into a dog, which, through his strength and instinct and cunning, is quickly able to master the law of club and fang, and then in the middle chapter of the novel, we saw Buck becoming the master of the entire dogsled team. In contrast, in the last half of the novel, we have seen him almost destroyed by the incompetency and ineptness of three people of the Southland – Hal, Charles, and Mercedes. In the last chapter, we saw proof of how thoroughly Buck became a creature of deep loyalty and admiration to a man fully deserving this devotion. This final chapter, then, will present yet another view of Buck: his complete reversion to the primitive, or in the terms of this novel, his final surrender to the "call of the wild."

Returning to the narrative, we realize anew that John Thornton is now in possession of sixteen hundred dollars. Thus, he and Pete and Hans are able to pay off their debts, which they do, and then the three of them take off in search of a fabled lost gold mine, a mine which many have heard of, and many have searched for, but most have died searching for it. Yet the legend of the lost mine persists: "Dying men had sworn to it . . . clinching their testimony with nuggets that were unlike any known grade of gold in the Northland."

Even though the lost mine might be fictitious, or nonexistent, yet John Thornton and Buck are delighted to start out on a journey through "infinite wandering in strange places." The search for the

lost gold mine is a traditional search which fills many adventure novels of Western literature; likewise, the search for the fabled Fountain
of Youth, as well as the search for the Holy Grail, are other quests
well known in Western literature. In each search, the participants
have to undergo many trials and tribulations, but it is the quest itself
that is, ultimately, as important as the discovery. In this particular
quest, Thornton, Hans, and Pete move farther and farther away from
civilization, and thus they are immersed deeper and deeper into
nature's primordial conditions. Meanwhile, Buck devotedly follows
his master in search of the lost gold mine, and, likewise, he is
brought closer and closer to the primordial wilderness and its
primitive existence.

As they travel, they almost always rely on their own ingenuity
for food, and when food is scarce, they go without. There is no alter-
native. Months pass, and, as London says, they "twisted through the
unchartered vastness where no men were." Once they do find the
shambles of an old hunting lodge, and there they find remnants that
indicate that other men have been here before. Then, in the spring,
they find the place where the large, legendary gold nuggets are supposed to be. The men pan for gold, and, in London's words, "they
heaped the treasure up." Buck spends many long hours close to the
fire, and he remembers the "short-legged hairy man" who appeared
in Chapter 3. The overwhelming memory which Buck has of this
hairy man concerns Buck's being constantly frightened and, along
with the memory of this ape-like figure, is the call of the wild, a call
which Buck constantly hears in the forest. It causes strange and unknown feelings to rise within him. He is aware of some kind of primitive yearnings which he cannot identify. Employing the philosophy
of Naturalism, London is apparently trying to juxtapose the dream of
the "ape man" as being symbolic of the primitive element in all
humankind; thus, this figure represents a kind of primitive ancestor
calling to Buck, imploring him to respond and to return to the call of
the wild.

After his dream of the hairy man, Buck becomes ever more en-
tranced by the call of the wild. It becomes, finally, almost irresisti-
ble. Sometimes, according to London, Buck springs up from sleeping
with a start, and from the forest, he hears a long-drawn howl, ". . .
unlike any noise made by a husky dog." One time, he even follows
the sound and comes upon an open place in a grove where he sees a

lean timber wolf howling at the sky. Buck is much larger than this wolf, and so he chases the wolf into "one blind channel" after another, but he does so only to let the wolf know that he intends it no harm. Afterward, running through the woods with the wolf, Buck knows at last that he is answering "the call," running side-by-side with his "wood brother." It is almost as if he feels that he has done the same thing before – but in another world – "now only a dim memory."

In the midst of his re-introduction and re-immersion into the wilderness, however, Buck suddenly stops and remembers John Thornton, and he retraces his steps back to the camp where he finds John Thornton amused by Buck's actions. These scenes are, of course, showing Buck constantly fluctuating between being a part of civilization, as represented by Thornton, and concomitantly, showing the fascinating lure of the "call of the wild," represented by the baying of wild wolves.

Buck fluctuates; he spends a couple of days in camp with John Thornton, and then suddenly he becomes restless, and once again, he takes to wandering in the woods. Then, more and more, he stays away from the camp for days at a time. In the wilderness, he wanders about seeking signs of his "wild brother" – the wolf. He fishes for salmon, and, at one point, he even kills a large black bear because feelings have been aroused in him which are latent remnants of the primitive and the ferocious.

When he returns to the remnants of the bear two days later, he discovers a dozen wolverines at the spoil. The wolverines scatter at Buck's arrival, except for two bold ones, which he kills. After this, Buck's "blood longing becomes stronger. . . . He was a killer, a thing that preyed . . . surviving triumphantly in a hostile environment where only the strong survived." Because of Buck's Saint Bernard father, he had inherited a size and a weight far greater than that of the wolf, and from Buck's shepherd mother, he had inherited an intelligence and a cunning which became a "wolf cunning." Buck is almost transformed into a wild animal in the peak of condition – strong, powerful, cunning, vigorous, and alert. As John Thornton says, "Never was there such a dog."

Buck is now ready to complete his transformation from his previous civilized life to the ways of the wilderness. Whereas he was previously a devoted "friend" to John Thornton, he is now a wild creature who has learned to live by his own cunning and intelligence. Whereas earlier, he could kill any time he wanted to, he does not kill from "wantonness," cruelty, nor simply for the wild pleasure of it; he kills only when he needs food for his own preservation. Earlier, even when he was not hungry, he would practice those skills which he had already mastered – that is, he would trap various types of animals, simply for the thrill of trapping them, and then he would let them escape from him. Once, seeing a band of twenty moose, Buck chooses one exceptionally large buck, and "guided by that instinct which came from the old hunting days of the primordial world," Buck decides to stalk him, and while doing so, he notices that this particular animal has been wounded; it has a feathered arrow embedded just "forward of the flank," which causes the moose to be particularly savage. Each time that Buck lures the old moose from the rest of the herd, a younger bull moose comes to the aid of their old leader. At such moments, though, Buck merely lures him on and stalks him with the patience of the wild, a patience that is "dogged, tireless, persistent, as life itself." After awhile, the younger bulls give up their protection of the old leader, realizing that it is more important to get the entire herd down to lower pasturelands. From that moment on, both night and day, Buck constantly stalks his prey, in a relentless manner, never permitting it to relax. At the end of the fourth day, Buck finally pulls the great moose down, and after enjoying the kill, he feels refreshed and renewed and decides to find John Thornton's camp.

London's purpose in having Buck kill the wolverines and his stalking and killing the moose is to let the reader know that Buck has now totally mastered the ways of the wilderness; from now on, Buck will be able to survive in the wild without any help from human beings.

Returning to camp, Buck discovers a fresh trail which creates suspicion in him. Thus, he approaches the camp with a great deal of caution; there, he finds Nig, one of Thornton's dogs, lying dead from an arrow's poisoning. Farther on, Buck finds another of Thornton's dogs dead. Creeping cautiously on his belly, Buck finds the camp in shambles, and "for the last time in his life he allowed passion to usurp cunning and reason" – all because of his great love for John Thornton. Suddenly, he sees the reason for the bloody chaos: the Yeehats, a band of ferocious Indians. Without caution, he begins to attack one Indian after another, tearing out their throats. His newly untamed ferocity continues until all of the Yeehats are seized with panic and flee in terror, thinking that they have seen the Great Evil Spirit.

Buck pursues the Indians briefly, then returns to the camp, where he finds Pete dead in his blankets and then he discovers Thornton's body half-submerged in water. As Buck surveys the carnage of the camp, he realizes a strange pride—greater than any he had yet experienced: "he had killed man, the noblest game of all, and he had killed in the face of the law of club and fang." Thus, the story has come full circle: in the first chapter, when the man in the red sweater taught Buck that a man with a club would always be the master of an animal, Buck now has proven himself to be superior to men—even men with arrows and spears and clubs.

When Buck attacked, the *men* fled in terror. And now that John Thornton is dead, Buck has no more ties with civilization. So, as Buck stands in the center of the camp site, a great open space, he realizes that all of his ties to civilization are broken, and he hears again "the many-noted call of the wild," which sounds more luring and compelling than ever before.

When a pack of wolves moves close to the camp, one of the large wolves attempts to attack Buck, and the wolf is immediately killed. Three others attack and withdraw, streaming with blood from slashed shoulders and throats. The entire pack, then, pins Buck down so that he cannot escape, and he is forced to fight the entire pack alone. At this point, one of the wolves advances cautiously, and in a friendly manner, he touches his nose to Buck's. It is the wolf that Buck had run with earlier. Buck has now become a member of the wolf pack, and, as London says, he "ran with them side by side . . . yelping as he ran."

London closes the novel by telling us that Buck becomes mythic in proportion, and a legend spreads from generation to generation. The rumor becomes so widespread, in fact, that the valley where Buck first encountered the Yeehats becomes known as the home of the Great Evil Spirit, and no one dares to approach that valley. Furthermore, over the years, Buck creates a new breed of animal—marked with light patches of hair, which is, of course, inherited from Buck. Buck has truly answered the call of the wild; the civilized animal has become the leader of a pack of wolves. The call of the wild has been heard, and it has been answered magnificently.

QUESTIONS FOR REVIEW

1. What does London mean by the title *The Call of the Wild*?

2. Discuss how the title of each chapter applies both to that chapter and to the general theme of the novel. For example, what is meant by naming certain chapters "The Toil of Trace and Trail," "Into the Primitive," and "The Dominant Primordial Beast"?

3. What influence did the "man in the red sweater" have on Buck's life?

4. How is Buck affected by the various masters that he has?

5. In the case of Charles and Hal, can a brutal man effectively train a dog?

6. Discuss London's use of anthropomorphism – that is, how London assigns human feelings and emotions to the various dogs.

7. Compare and contrast the life of the North with the life represented by the Southland.

8. How does Jack London's first-hand knowledge of life in the North add to the reality of the novel?

9. Trace Buck's change from being a civilized dog to being a complete product of the wilderness.

10. Why do you think London chose to have John Thornton massacred?

WHITE FANG

GENERAL PLOT SUMMARY

Part One of the novel shows two men, Henry and Bill, struggling to bring the corpse of Lord Alfred back to civilization. It is a time of famine, and they are low on food; also, they have little ammunition. Thus, they are in a desperate situation because they are being pursued by a pack of famished wolves. As the novel begins, they have six sled dogs, but one night, they notice that there are *seven* dogs to be fed. Strangely, the next morning, there are only *five* dogs to be fed. As a result, they become suspicious, and finally they notice a she-wolf who comes to the camp at night and lures the dogs away.

When the men have only two dogs left, Bill decides to shoot the she-wolf, but he is killed himself by the famished wolf pack. Thus Henry is left alone – with only two dogs and no ammunition – and after days of traveling, covering only a short distance each day, he is forced to build a fire to surround himself and protect himself from the wolves. When he awakens in the morning, he realizes immediately that his supply of wood is gone, and he cannot go out and search for some more. He resigns himself, therefore, to the inevitable, but he is finally rescued by a group of men who are also out in the wild.

Part Two of the novel shifts the narrative perspective to that of the she-wolf. After the famine is over, the wolf pack separates, and the she-wolf and three males travel together, until one of the wolves, "One Eye," kills the other two. The she-wolf and One Eye travel together, then, until it is time for her to settle down to give birth to her cubs. Another famine comes upon the land when the cubs are still young, and all of the cubs die – except one: a gray wolf cub. This gray wolf is the strongest and the most adventuresome of all the litter. Yet early in his life, he learns how to snare food and along with this, he learns the lesson of the wilderness – that is, "eat or be eaten, kill or be killed."

In Part Three, the cub and its mother wander into an Indian camp, where the mother is recognized by an Indian named Gray Beaver; she answers immediately to the call of "Kiche," and the little gray cub is promptly named White Fang. In the Indian camp, the cub has to learn how to function in the presence of the Indians, and he must also learn how to protect himself against the other puppies. When his mother is taken from him, he attempts to follow her, but he is severely beaten by Gray Beaver, and thus he quickly learns another lesson – to obey the "man-god." When Gray Beaver goes to the nearest fort to sell his furs, he takes White Fang with him. There at the fort, White Fang becomes famous for his ferocious ability to kill other dogs, and he is sought after by a vicious, ugly man named, ironically, Beauty Smith, who, by using trickery and alcohol, is able to trick Gray Beaver into selling White Fang to him. White Fang is treated terribly by this cruel man; he is constantly forced into bloody fights with other dogs so that Smith can win bets. But during one fight with a bulldog, White Fang is at the point of being killed when a man named Weedon Scott, a person of distinction and authority, interferes and stops the fight. Furthermore, Scott pays off Beauty Smith and threatens to have him jailed. Scott then takes White Fang with him.

Under the protection and patience and compassion of Weedon Scott, White Fang gradually learns to appreciate a human being, and ultimately he comes to possess a love and affection for Scott.

When Weeden Scott has to return to his home in the Southland (California), he at first intends to leave White Fang behind. White Fang, however, escapes and sneaks aboard the ship. Scott, therefore, chooses to take the dog along. The novel ends by showing how White Fang learns to exist as a domesticated animal. Ultimately, White Fang wins the affection of Scott's family because of his extreme intelligence (for example, he leads some men to help his injured master) and also because of his performing an act of bravery by risking his life to save Judge Scott from being murdered.

LIST OF CHARACTERS

The following human beings appear in the book:

Gray Beaver

The Indian who first owns Kiche, White Fang's mother, and the man who later owns White Fang. Gray Beaver represents a type of impersonal master in White Fang's life. As such, he will stand in contrast to such savage owners as Beauty Smith and such compassionate owners as Weedon Scott. Essentially, Gray Beaver respects White Fang because he is a dog of many uses. Because of this, Gray Beaver is quite willing to give White Fang food, protection, and shelter in exchange for White Fang's obedience and work. When Gray Beaver comes under the addiction of alcohol, he exchanges White Fang to the vicious and cruel Beauty Smith—simply to get whiskey.

Kloo-kooch

Gray Beaver's squaw.

Mit-sah

Gray Beaver's son; he is responsible for training White Fang for the fan-like trace.

Beauty Smith

A vicious, evil man, extremely hideous in appearance; London calls him a "monstrosity." His outer hideousness represents the corruption of his soul. Smith, who is hated by the world, uses White Fang as an object through which he vents his own hatred. He seems to take an inner satisfaction out of deliberately tormenting White Fang physically, with jabs and punches and whips, or else tormenting White Fang mentally, with derision and laughter. He uses the dog only to gain money; otherwise, he does not respond to the dog.

Tim Keenan

The owner of a bulldog named Cherokee. When Cherokee and White Fang fight, Keenan is somewhat of a passive onlooker, and he is not resentful when Weedon Scott breaks up the fight between the two dogs.

Weedon Scott

He is the most important character in the novel because he represents the compassionate, humane, and kind human being who, through patience and understanding, is able to transform White Fang from a wild beast into a civilized animal. He is the only one who understands that an animal needs more than just to be fed – that it also needs attention and love. In return for his companionship and love, White Fang gives Scott his complete love and devotion; he is totally obedient to him.

Matt

Weedon Scott's assistant; even though Matt is in charge of feeding White Fang every day, White Fang's total allegiance belongs to Weedon Scott.

Judge Scott and Alice Scott

Weedon Scott's parents; they own a huge estate in the Sierra Vista Valley in California.

Beth Scott

Weedon Scott's sister.

Jim Hall

An incorrigible villain; he kills three guards and escapes from San Quentin. White Fang saves Judge Scott's life when Hall tries to murder the Judge.

Bill and Henry

Two sled drivers who appear in the first section of the novel, before White Fang is born.

The following animals play an important role in this novel and have characteristics very similar to those of human beings (called anthropomorphism).

White Fang

This dog is actually three-fourths wolf and one part dog. He possesses all of the intelligence of the dog family, along with the quickness and the slyness of the wolf family. From his very first weeks, White Fang proves that he is the strongest of the litter; he survives a famine that kills his brothers and sisters. Later, he gains a reputation for being one of the most savage dogs in the North. However, under the tutelage of a gentle master, White Fang eventually develops into a civilized animal.

Kiche

The she-wolf who appears in the first part of the novel; she lures sled dogs away from the team of Henry and Bill. She is later the mother of White Fang.

One Eye

An old scarred wolf hound who sires White Fang.

Lip-lip

One of the dogs in Gray Beaver's camp; he makes life miserable for the younger and smaller White Fang.

Cherokee

A bulldog belonging to Tim Keenan; he almost kills White Fang before Weedon Scott separates them.

Collie

A female sheep-dog whose initial animosity towards White Fang is equalled only by her later passion for him.

Dick

Judge Scott's loyal and gentle deer-hound.

SUMMARIES AND COMMENTARIES

Part One

As background knowledge for a full understanding of the novel *White Fang*, the reader should be familiar with London's earlier and equally famous novel, *The Call of the Wild* (1903). While London did not intend these novels to be sequential, or that one should follow another, there is, nevertheless, a thematic relationship that exists between the two. For example, in the earlier novel *The Call of the Wild*, London treats the matter of a civilized dog's being converted to the ways of the wild in the primitive North. At the end of the novel, the previously civilized dog has become wild, and he has sired a new strain of wild dogs, a breed that is part dog and part wild wolf. In contrast, the novel *White Fang* (1906) begins with a previously tamed dog seen in his native habitat, functioning as a wild beast. In the first three chapters, this animal is simply referred to as a "she-wolf." We are not implying that London deliberately conceived this novel as a continuation of the preceding novel, but merely that he is using a situation analogous to that in the earlier novel.

Even though the first three chapters of *White Fang* are referred to as Part One, they have very little to do with the succeeding chapters of the book. For example, Henry and Bill are never heard of again, and Lord Alfred's corpse is left suspended in the tree. As is often the case with many novels, a certain portion of a novel can be published as a separate entity, and these first three chapters (in Part One) stand so independently from the rest of the novel that they can be looked upon as a separate short story.

However, in relationship to the entirety of the novel *White Fang*, these chapters do present dramatically and forcefully the desolation and isolation against which the main body of the novel is set. In other words, the reader is introduced rather dramatically to the harsh, frozen Northland, where all types of life struggle desperately for mere existence.

Thus, the novel opens with two men, Henry and Bill, struggling against the "Wild, the savage, frozen-hearted Northland Wild." The scene is made even more eerie by the nature of their journey – that is, they are trying to return to civilization, Fort McGurry, with the dead body of Lord Alfred, a man whom we know little about, except that his family is considerably wealthy. As the men struggle against the elements, the eerie, ghostly presence of Lord Alfred in his coffin becomes more dominant. The two men are also in serious trouble because they are being constantly pursued by a large pack of gaunt, starving wolves. The wolves are so desperate for food that they eventually venture within a few yards of the camp site. Moreover, the men are at yet another disadvantage because they have only three cartridges left for their gun, and they are thus unable to shoot at random at the wolves. Therefore, every night, the two men have to build a roaring fire, or else they will be immediately devoured by the starving, desperate wolves.

About the man in the "oblong box" – Lord Alfred – London tells us little, except that Lord Alfred was a man whom "the Wild had conquered and beaten down until he would never move nor struggle again." We are told that the reason for this is that it "is not the way of the Wild to like movement."

Each night as the two men build the campfire to keep the wolves away, they can gradually sense the wolves growing bolder and bolder as their starvation increases. Then, one night, Bill goes out with six salmon to feed the six dogs, and he comes back totally perplexed because there were *seven* dogs instead of six to be fed. The next morning, however, there are only *five* dogs waiting to be fed – two dogs have seemingly disappeared. Soon they discover, at a distance, a she-wolf that was brazen enough to lure one of the male dogs away from the camp. Then, after the dog was lured away from the protective camp site, the wolf pack attacked it and totally devoured it – all because of their intense hunger. During the mysterious disappearance of the dogs, the presence of the coffin begins to prey on the two men's active imaginations. The presence of the coffin and the desolation and the extremely harsh weather cause the men to question their own sanity – for example, if the seventh animal the night before *had* been a wolf, it seems only logical that the dogs would have "pitched into it." But they didn't; therefore, the seventh "dog" *has* to be familiar with the ways of civilized man.

The next morning, when they realize that another dog, Fatty, is gone, they are not too concerned because Fatty was not a very bright dog anyway. However, "no fool dog ought to be fool enough to go off and commit suicide that way." The next night as they are making camp, the same thing happens again. The she-wolf appears and takes half of a salmon from Bill's hand before he recognizes the she-wolf as being a strange dog and can drive it away with a club. Later that night, however, a second dog, Frog, the strongest, is lured away and devoured by the wolf pack. The third night, Bill is determined that they will not lose another dog, and therefore, he contrives a method by which he ties a dog to a stick in such a way that the restraining leather strap cannot be chewed away. The next morning, though, another dog – Spanker – is gone. His strap has been gnawed through.

Henry and Bill assume that it was probably the dog next to Spanker, One Ear, that gnawed through the strap. London, however, implies that it was the she-wolf herself who gnawed through the leather strap, releasing Spanker. Bill then decides that he will tie the dogs out of reach of each other that night, because he notes that if it *was* the wolves who gnawed Spanker loose, they were so hungry that they ate even the leather strap that was tied to Spanker.

At this point, Bill becomes desperately angry over the manner in which the she-wolf is able to lure their dogs away from the camp, and he decides that the only solution is to use one of the three cartridges left; he must at least *try* to destroy the she-wolf. When they first see the wolf in the daylight, they observe that its coat is a "true wolf coat"—that is, the dominant color is gray, but there is a faint reddish-hue to the coat that indicates that the animal is not a full-blooded wolf. In fact, it looks "for all the world like a big husky sled dog." When Bill raises his rifle to get a good shot at the she-wolf, she immediately notices the weapon and darts for shelter.

When the fourth dog, One Ear, is lured away from the sled by the she-wolf, he and the other two remaining dogs were not, by coincidence, leashed to the sled because of an accident. Bill again decides that he must try to kill the she-wolf.

Meanwhile, One Ear, after declining to pursue the lure of the she-wolf, starts to head back to the protection of the men and the sled, but he is cut off by the pack of wolves, and he cannot get far enough ahead of the pack to cut through to the safety of the sled. Suddenly, Henry hears one shot followed quickly by two more in rapid succession, and he knows that the wolves have set upon One Ear and Bill.

Henry now realizes that he is completely alone, with only two dogs and *no ammunition.* So, using a man-harness, Henry, along with the two remaining dogs, begins to pull the sled. Before long, it becomes necessary to discard the heavy coffin bearing Lord Alfred, thus making the load considerably lighter. Each night, Henry stops well before dark in order to build two huge fires, but when he begins to doze off, he awakens to find that the wolves have crept up to within a couple of yards from him. Because Henry has on such heavy protective gloves, he is able to plunge his hands into the bed of coals and toss the glowing embers onto the wolves, thus frightening them off. This continues for many nights, until finally one morning, at daylight, the wolves refuse to retreat, thus forcing Henry and his two dogs to spend the entire day by the fire. He cannot even leave the fire long enough so that he can cut enough wood to kindle a fire; thus, he has to build a trail of fires to the nearby woods, where there are several dead trees which he can chop down.

One night, exhausted from lack of sleep, he awakens to find himself completely surrounded by wolves – "the teeth of one had closed upon his arm" – and he instinctively leaps into the fire and begins throwing live coals at his attackers. He then builds a circle of fire around him and sits on his blanket to protect himself from the wolves. Gradually, his supply of wood begins to disappear, and there seems no way for him to replenish his dwindling supply. Exhausted even further from lack of sleep, he resigns himself to the inevitable: he lies down and goes to sleep, only to be awakened by a "mysterious change that had taken place." He discovers that the wolves have disappeared, and he is now surrounded by several dog sleds and a half dozen men. One of the men asks about Lord Alfred, and Henry tells him that Lord Alfred is dead, and that his body is still "roosting in the tree at the last camp."

One of London's goals in this chapter is to show the constant conflict between man and primitive beasts, and, at the same time, to allow the reader to know that the animals are extremely cunning in their savagery – as can be seen particularly in the way that the she-wolf is able to lure off the male dogs, one by one. As noted at the beginning of this discussion, the desolation and the isolation of the wilderness is in direct conflict with the intelligence of man. Bill tries to destroy the animals, and he fails, and Henry has to use all of his native intelligence in order to survive the onslaught of the pack of wolves. The ending of this section is, however, melodramatic, since Henry is miraculously saved at a moment when all hope of escape has been abandoned. The reading audience of 1906, however, was enthusiastic, and they loved such melodramatic endings.

Part Two

This part of the novel reverts backward in time, and, in addition, it makes a shift in the narrative point of view so that we now see events from the viewpoint of the she-wolf. It is not until Part Three of the novel, however, that we discover the name of the she-wolf –

"Kiche" – and discover that the she-wolf was once a tame animal that now belongs to an Indian named Gray Beaver. Instead, Part Two concerns itself with showing the she-wolf in her own environment with a pack of wild wolves. In Part One, we saw that when the wolf pack was closing in on Henry for the kill, and that when the other men came to the rescue, "the pack was loath to forego the kill it had hunted down." In a like fashion, they work together as a group tracking down a big bull moose, and London gives the reader a vivid description of the manner in which the wolf pack stalks and kills the bull moose.

After the pack is driven away, they break into smaller packs, and each pack goes its own way. At this time, the she-wolf attracts three males to her, one a very young three-year-old, who has just attained his adulthood, the second a mature wolf, and the third an old one-eyed wolf, tattered from many fights.

There is famine in the land, and as long as the wolf pack works together, they survive, but as soon as the famine is over, fights begin for the attentions of the she-wolf, and the inexperienced three-year-old is attacked by the old one-eyed wolf and the mature wolf, and the two quickly destroy him. Then the old one-eyed wolf, using his experience and trickery, catches the other wolf off-guard and kills him. He is now the sole companion of the she-wolf. Significantly, the she-wolf seems pleased by the death battles for her attention.

Together now, the two wolves roam the countryside stalking game, and it is the she-wolf who teaches the old wolf how to raid Indian traps. After some time, however, the she-wolf begins to grow "heavy and restless," and she begins to search for a nesting place where she can give birth to her litter. She finally finds a place under a rocky crag, close to a river in a cave that gives her protection on three sides.

One day, when the old one-eyed wolf comes back from a day of hunting, he pauses at the mouth of the cave, and he is surprised by the "remotely familiar" sounds and finds five young wolf cubs in the nest. Since this is not the first time that he has been a father, he understands what has happened. Likewise, when he approaches the cubs and is violently repulsed by the she-wolf, he accepts the rebuke knowingly. The she-wolf, "in her instinct," knew that male wolves had often "eaten their new-born and helpless progeny." The old one-eyed wolf accepts his new role and position, which is now, for the most part, to go out and forage for food and bring it back to the female, who then feeds it to her cubs.

Another famine, however, is soon upon the countryside, and the male wolf cannot find food for his family. He tries to kill a porcupine, which protects itself by rolling into a ball; later that day, the old wolf comes upon a ptarmigan bird, which he kills, and out of instinct begins to eat – then, remembering his duty, he carries the ptarmigan back to the den. Another time, he watches a female lynx, but he knows that she is too dangerous to allow herself to be attacked and killed. As he watches the lynx, though, he sees it give the porcupine a death blow, but before the porcupine dies, it wounds the lynx sufficiently enough to drive it away; consequently, old One Eye is able to wait until the porcupine dies and then carry it back to the lair.

The she-wolf's instinctive fear of the father of her progeny is abating; "he was behaving as a wolf father should." Meanwhile, one gray cub is drifting away from his brothers and sisters. The others, coincidentally, seem to have a trace of fur which indicates that they are closer to the domestically raised mother in their *instincts*, whereas, in contrast, the gray cub seems to be related closer to the pure wolf stock. Furthermore, the gray cub is the fiercest and most adventuresome of the litter.

In the time of the great famine, when there is no more meat, and there is no more milk from the mother's breasts, the other cubs die from starvation. Only the gray cub is left – due to his natural superiority. The survival of the gray cub is a reiteration of London's theme concerning "the survival of the fittest," nature's way of assuring the continuance of a species.

Sometime during the famine, old One Eye leaves, however, and never comes back. The cub cannot understand this, but the she-wolf knows, instinctively, that he has been killed by the lynx.

As the young cub grows, he becomes more adventuresome, and one time when the she-wolf is out hunting for food, the cub wanders out of the cave. But, as will often happen, without his knowing why, some instinctive fear drives him back into the shelter of the cave; this is a fear that is "the legacy of the wild which no animal may escape." On subsequent explorations outside of the cave, the cub gains more and more courage, and he travels farther and farther away from the lair. Once, by accident, he stumbles into a nest of baby ptarmigans. At first, he is frightened, and then his instincts take over, and, in London's words, the cub's "jaws closed . . . and there was a crunching of fragile bones and warm blood ran from his mouth. The taste of it was good." The gray cub eats the entire brood, and then, as he leaves the nest as a conqueror, he is suddenly attacked by the ptarmigan hen. "It was his first battle. He was elated. . . . he was no longer afraid of anything." But he is about to lose the battle, when, by a stroke of luck, a great hawk suddenly swoops down and snatches up the mother ptarmigan and carries her away, thus saving the gray cub from certain death. It is a good learning lesson for him: kill or be killed. It is the law of the wild. Exploring farther, the gray cub falls into a river and almost drowns before he is able to crawl out. Thus he learns another lesson about survival – water *can* be dangerous.

The gray cub next comes upon a young weasel, which is so small that the little cub begins to play with it. Suddenly, however, the mother weasel appears, and even though she is even smaller than the gray cub, the cub quickly discovers that she is savage and fierce, and that she would have killed him had not the cub's mother, the she-wolf, appeared just in time to save him.

The cub develops rapidly, but then there comes a famine upon the land, and the she-wolf runs herself thin in search of meat. The famine becomes so terrible, in fact, that the she-wolf becomes desperate – so desperate, in fact, that she is finally forced to raid the nest of the lynx, knowing full well that the lynx is a vicious animal and is fully capable of killing her. Nevertheless, she raids the lynx's nest and brings back the four lynx kittens, and she and her gray cub devour them. The mother lynx, not unsurprisingly, comes to the she-wolf's lair for revenge, and the she-wolf is no match for the powerful lynx until the young gray cub rushes forward and sinks his teeth into the hind legs of the lynx. This so hampers the lynx that, together, the mother and her cub are able to kill the fierce lynx. However, during the battle, the cub's shoulder is ripped to the bone, and the she-wolf is wounded almost to the point of death. From this encounter, the gray cub learns this lesson: "the aim of life was meat. Life itself was meat. Life lived on life. There were the eaters and the eaten. The law WAS EAT OR BE EATEN."

Basically, this part of the novel focuses on the lessons which the gray cub learns – that is, eat or be eaten, or, in simple ecological terms, animals kill other animals for food. Also in this chapter,

London gives us a vivid picture of many aspects of life in the wilderness, and not only does he show us the savagery with which one animal kills another animal for food, but he also shows us how a mother wolf, or a mother ptarmigan, a mother weasel, or a mother lynx, will endanger themselves in order to protect their offspring. Part of the law of the wilderness, therefore, is that of *instinct* – which the gray cub quickly learns and develops.

By extension, London is using his own philosophy of Naturalism, believing that man is a victim of a hostile universe. Therefore, in this novel, London shows us that in the wilderness, as well as in the life of civilized man, all is "blindness and confusion. . . . violence and disorder, the chaos of gluttony and slaughter, ruled over by chance [which is] merciless, planless, endless."

Part Three

Whereas Part Two focused on an animal surviving in the wilderness by primitive instinct, Part Three will now reverse this trend and will essentially show the gray cub (White Fang) beginning to learn a more difficult lesson – that of surviving in a civilized society, where he will have to learn to live among men – and friendly dogs. (Whereas *Call of the Wild* showed us how Buck moved from a comfortable and easy life in civilization into an environment in which he had to learn how to survive in the primitive world, this will be a reversal of that idea.)

White Fang's life in the Indian camp becomes daily more intolerable – principally because of the constant persecution of Lip-lip, who somehow manages to turn all the other dogs against White Fang. For example, whenever White Fang ventures away from Kiche, he is savagely attacked by Lip-lip. Consequently, he never has a chance to allow the genial, playful, "puppy-ish" side of his nature to find expression. He has to be constantly alert to the dangers represented by Lip-lip. But even though Lip-lip is a larger dog, White Fang can run more swiftly, and one time he engages Lip-lip in a chase, and as they dart in and out of the camp, White Fang deceptively leads Lip-lip past Kiche, who, although she is tied up, is able to grab Lip-lip and repeatedly rip and slash him with her fangs. Then, taking advantage of Lip-lip's weakened condition, White Fang sinks his teeth into

Lip-lip's hind leg, and he would have destroyed Lip-lip had not the Indians driven him away.

One day, Gray Beaver decides that Kiche will probably not try to escape, and so he releases her. White Fang is delighted with his mother's new freedom, and time and again, he tries to lead her away from the Indian camp. He runs out toward the wilderness, and she follows, but eventually she always returns to the Indian camp. Thus, we see that "the call of the wild" is not as strong in White Fang as is the *call of his mother*, for he always follows her back. Apparently, Kiche has found an element of contentment in the protection of the man-animals and does not wish to leave them.

It is at this point that White Fang is confronted with his most difficult lesson. Gray Beaver owes a debt to another Indian – Three Eagles – and in order to settle the debt, Gray Beaver gives Kiche to him. When Three Eagles leaves in his canoe, along with Kiche, White Fang tries to follow, swimming after the canoe, in spite of the fact that Gray Beaver sternly commands him to return to camp. It is unpardonable not to obey the commands of the man-gods, and White Fang learns this lesson when Gray Beaver gets into his canoe and pursues White Fang downriver, picking him up, and giving him one fierce blow after another – until White Fang lies almost unconscious, limp in the bottom of the canoe. Then Gray Beaver kicks White Fang out of his way. In retaliation, White Fang bites Gray Beaver, and White Fang learns a lesson that he never forgets. As a result of his biting Gray Beaver, White Fang receives a very severe beating from Gray Beaver – and never again, regardless of the circumstances, does he bite "the god who was lord and master over him."

Lip-lip, seeing White Fang in such a weakened condition, takes advantage of this opportunity to attack him, and White Fang, of course, is too weak to defend himself and would have been destroyed by Lip-lip if Gray Beaver had not been there to defend White Fang. Thus, White Fang learns another lesson – that is, his lord and master is also his protector.

Now that White Fang is totally alone – without his mother's protection – Lip-lip uses this opportunity to encourage the other dogs to become constant and fierce enemies of White Fang. As a result, White Fang becomes a total outcast. From this constant persecution of the entire pack, White Fang learns two important things: (1) how to defend himself against a mass attack by other dogs; and (2) how to inflict the greatest amount of damage upon another dog in the shortest length of time. In London's emphasis upon White Fang's being the total outcast, he is preparing us for White Fang's later, total alienation from all living beings, particularly in his later relationship with Beauty Smith, so that White Fang's final transformation into a civilized animal under the care of Weedon Scott will be as dramatic as possible.

At present, throughout this part of the novel, the emphasis will continue to be on White Fang, as a single entity, pitted against a hostile universe, comprised of both man and animal.

It is surprising that White Fang never runs away from the Indian camp, even though he is not accepted in the camp, and even though he is in constant fights against overwhelming odds. He hangs tenaciously onto his position in the camp and to Gray Beaver, although Gray Beaver will never be the "perfect master" that Weedon Scott will prove to be. By defending himself, White Fang becomes, in London's words, "hated by man and dog." White Fang steals food wherever and whenever possible; he slyly attacks other dogs when they are off guard, and, ultimately, he becomes the terror of the camp, as well as the scapegoat of the camp. He is blamed for all of the camp's hardships—particularly by the squaws.

Being part wild, however, White Fang is always able to outrun the other dogs, and, therefore, he is able to escape any injury that might be inflicted by the other dogs. According to London, White Fang is "hated by his kind and by mankind . . . his development was rapid and one-sided." Throughout his growth, though, he proves that he can learn to obey the strong and oppress the weak. Consequently, he obeys Gray Beaver, whom he sees as a god, and he attacks anything which is weaker or smaller than he is.

One fall, sometime after Kiche's leaving, the Indians break camp in order to go on a hunting expedition, but White Fang deliberately decides to stay behind. So, as Gray Beaver and his family are leaving, White Fang hides in a dense thicket and refuses to answer the call of his master's voice. Each time he hears Gray Beaver's voice calling him, he trembles with fear, but he refuses to answer. After the Indians have left, White Fang relishes in his new-found freedom, and he romps and plays in the forest. By nightfall, however, he becomes aware of a loneliness and of a "lurking of danger unseen and unguessed." Furthermore, he is cold and hungry, and it is then that he realizes that there is no one to feed him, and that there is no place to steal food from, nor even a comfortable place to sleep. Suddenly, his hunger, his loneliness, and his fear make him realize his mistake. A panic seizes him, and he immediately begins to search for Gray Beaver's camp. He runs downstream in the direction which the Indians took, and he would never have found Gray Beaver had it not been for the fact that Gray Beaver and his family were camping separately from the other Indians, intent on tracking down a moose. Night has already fallen when White Fang discovers Gray Beaver's camp, and he crawls timidly on his belly into the camp, fully expecting to be beaten by Gray Breaver. White Fang trembles, waiting for his beating, and he is surprised when Gray Beaver brings some fresh meat to him from the moose which Gray Beaver has just killed. With this act, White Fang fully acknowledges that Gray Beaver is his master — "the god to whom he had given himself, and upon whom he was now dependent."

In December, Gray Beaver plans a trip up the Mackenzie River, and in order to carry all of his possessions, he gives to his son, Mit-sah, a small sled and tells him to have all of the puppies pull it. Because White Fang has seen other dogs pulling sleds, he does not resent being harnessed to the sled. The seven puppies for Mit-sah's sled are arranged in a fan-shaped team because they are too inexperienced to run in regular dogsled fashion, which is, of course, in single file. Interestingly, in Mit-sah's training the puppies, there is another advantage to this fan formation: the varying lengths of the ropes prevent the other dogs from attacking the dog immediately ahead of him. Yet Mit-sah, who has often observed Lip-lip's persecution of White Fang, decides to get revenge by placing Lip-lip at the front — at the apex of the fan-shaped team. Not only that, but Mit-sah gives Lip-lip extra meat rations so as to make the other dogs resentful of Lip-lip, and so that the other dogs, out of their extreme jealousy of Lip-lip, will attempt to attack him from the rear; therefore, they will pull the sled faster. Ultimately, though, *all* of the dogs turn against Lip-lip, mainly because of his mean temperament, and soon White Fang becomes the lead dog, and because of this, he becomes a tyrant over the other dogs.

Even though White Fang has an allegiance to Gray Beaver, and even though he acknowledges Gray Beaver's superiority, there is no love or affection between man and beast. However, at a village at Great Slave Lake, White Fang is foraging for food when he finds a young boy chopping some frozen moose meat. When White Fang begins to eat one of the frozen chips which has flown off the chopping block, the boy pursues White Fang, and he corners him and is about to kill him. Now White Fang must decide: he must either attack the "man-god," which is forbidden, or be killed himself. White Fang's "sense of justice" forces him to bite the boy in order to preserve his own (White Fang's) life. When the boy's family demands vengeance, Gray Beaver, supported by Mit-sah and Kloo-kooch, defends White Fang. It is at this time that White Fang learns that "justice and injustice" vary according to the man-gods.

That same day, White Fang learns more about the man-gods' laws of justice. When Mit-sah is gathering firewood out in the forest near Great Slave Lake, an injured boy and some of his friends descend on Mit-sah and beat him severely. For awhile, White Fang does nothing – until he realizes that Mit-sah is being "unjustly" attacked. At that moment, White Fang leaps among the attackers and scatters them, thus saving Mit-sah from any further beating. For this action, for White Fang's having rescued his son, Gray Beaver awards White Fang with an extra ration of fresh meat. From these experiences, White Fang learns about the laws of property and when to defend Gray Beaver's property against other "man-gods." White Fang now realizes that he has made a covenant with Gray Beaver. In exchange for his own liberty, White Fang receives fire, food, companionship, protection, and in return, he gives his complete allegiance to Gray Beaver.

The following April, White Fang develops more fully in stature and growth. He is now one year old, and he is large enough to hold his own against any other dog. For example, a test of White Fang's growing maturity occurs when an old dog, Baseek, tries to usurp some of White Fang's food. Yet, while White Fang is growing stronger, Baseek is growing weaker, and neither can be sure what the other might do if they were to square off against each other. Note here that if Baseek had held his ground, White Fang would have retreated, but when White Fang sees the old dog about to devour meat which White Fang wants, he reacts savagely, and he drives the old dog away. This gives White Fang "a faith in himself and a greater pride."

That summer, White Fang has another unique experience. While investigating a new tepee, he suddenly comes upon Kiche, his mother, whom he has not seen in some time. In London's words, "He *remembered* her vaguely, but he *remembered* her." Kiche, however, as is the custom with wolf-mothers, is concerned now *only* with her new litter of cubs, and she viciously drives White Fang away. White Fang is confused, but his instincts tell him that he can never attack a female of his kind.

Here, London interrupts the story of White Fang for a moment to make an authorial comment about the nature of White Fang's development. London always believed that environment affects an animal (be it man, or dog, or wolf), and in this case, London points out that environment has molded White Fang into more of a dog than a wolf. Had White Fang not come into contact with man, White Fang would have developed along the lines of his heredity — that is, he would have matured into a true wolf. London individualizes White Fang by assigning him uniquely human qualities. For example, he says of White Fang: "He could not stand being laughed at." This quality is emphasized strongly, and it will become a key to the animosity which will exist between him and Beauty Smith.

When White Fang is three years old, there occurs another great famine. This particular famine, however, is so intense that "only the strong survived." Gray Beaver and his family, in desperation, have to resort to eating the "soft-tanned leather of their moccasins and mittens." As for the dogs, they begin to eat one another, and, finally, even the man-gods eat the worthless and weaker dogs. At this time, White Fang realizes that he can no longer rely on the man-gods for food and protection; therefore, he quietly steals away into the forest and resorts to hunting, which is his nature, his instinct. Alone, he is able to track down a young wolf and devour it. He also encounters again his mother, Kiche, who has had another litter of pups, of which there is only one left, and, as before, White Fang leaves Kiche and her pup alone and does not disturb them. His hunger is so great, though, that he raids one of Gray Beaver's traps, eating the rabbit which he finds there, even though he knows that Gray Beaver himself is starving. In contrast, White Fang has been lucky in his search for food, and thus he is in splendid condition (". . . he was even gorged from his latest kill") when he suddenly comes face-to-face with Lip-lip, his most hated enemy. There is no *real* contest, however. White Fang attacks Lip-lip and quickly drives his teeth into Lip-lip's scrawny throat. Then sometime later, he hears the sights and sounds of the Indian camp, and he realizes that the famine is over, for he smells food and hears pleasant noises. As a result, he returns to Gray Beaver's tepee to await Gray Beaver's return.

Essentially, then, Part Three deals with White Fang's relationship with man, particularly with White Fang's looking on man as some sort of god. White Fang feels subservient to this creature of greater intelligence, and he is willing to voluntarily return to this superior intelligence of his own volition after the famine is over. London seems to imply here, however, as he will in Part Five of the novel, that, however wild an animal might be, under proper training and proper care, he *can* be trained to obey man's orders.

Part Four

Whereas White Fang has never been liked by the other dogs, now that he has been made leader of Mit-sah's team, the other dogs develop an intense hatred for him, a hatred based on the fact that White Fang is the lead dog, in charge of discipline among the other dogs, and also because he is given an extra ration of meat by Mit-sah. White Fang takes great pride in his leadership, yet at the same time, he dislikes the other dogs' always "yapping" at his heels, knowing that if he ever slows down, they will be upon him in a minute. The pride of leadership, though, is modified by the fact that White Fang is once again keenly isolated from the rest of the pack. Thus, he has to learn to stay at a distance, to stay in open spaces where he can outrun the other dogs, if necessary, and avoid fights and places where he can be trapped. As a result, White Fang becomes more and more adept at protecting himself.

The following summer, Gray Beaver takes White Fang to Fort Yukon, and it is there that White Fang sees his first white man. Rumors of "great gold fields" have brought large numbers of white men to the Yukon, and, consequently, Gray Beaver has come to the fort with great bundles of furs, mittens, and moccasins to sell. He expects to make a large profit on his goods, but never in his wildest imagination does he expect to make over a *thousand percent profit* — which he does.

White Fang notices a great deal of difference between the white men-gods and the Indian men-gods. The white men-gods are, seemingly, *all powerful*, so much so that Gray Beaver is, in comparison with them, like a child-god. But if the white gods are more powerful, their dogs are obviously weaker. Consequently, while Gray Beaver is selling his goods, White Fang entertains himself by fighting the dogs that have come North with the white men. According to London, "White Fang did not love his kind . . . and the killing of the white men's dogs was a diversion." Fresh from the soft Southland, these dogs are easy prey for a dog of White Fang's experience. Early in Part Four, then, London once again points out that White Fang *could* have developed differently – had Gray Beaver given him any measure of love and devotion, as Weedon Scott will indeed give White Fang later in the novel. But, in the absence of this kindly treatment, White Fang is "molded until he became what he was, morose and lonely, unloving, and ferocious, the enemy of all his kind."

London lets us know that the few white men who lived permanently in Fort Yukon were known as "Sour-doughs" because of their using sour dough starter to make their own bread, and they look down on the newcomers who bring baking powder with them. These older men who look down on the new men are also obviously delighted with the way that White Fang dominates the dogs of the new arrivals.

One of these men is nicknamed "Beauty" Smith – actually he is "preeminently ugly" and, in fact, he is, in London's words, a "monstrosity." In addition, his outer nature is symbolic of his inner nature, probably because he is "the weakest of the weak-kneed and snivelling cowards." Unfortunately, however, as soon as Beauty Smith develops a liking for White Fang, particularly because of the dog's ability to fight in a savage manner, he is determined to purchase him. At this same time, White Fang develops an instinctive hatred for Beauty Smith.

Beauty Smith offers to buy the dog, but because Gray Beaver has made such a huge profit from his sales, he refuses – at first – to sell White Fang. "But Beauty Smith knew the ways of Indians," says London, and so Smith often takes bottles of whiskey to Gray Beaver's camp. Here, London is using a basic cliche about the Indians' drinking proclivities, a cliche which has, unfortunately, become commonplace today. At any rate, Gray Beaver soon becomes addicted to alcohol, and he squanders his entire profits upon whiskey. Now Beauty Smith is able to buy White Fang in exchange for whiskey.

The first time that White Fang is taken to Beauty Smith's house, he chews through the leather thong around his neck and returns to Gray Beaver. He escapes again, and again he resists being taken back to Smith's house, but he is beaten so brutally that he can hardly walk. Finally, after White Fang escapes a third time, Beauty Smith retrieves him and beats him so severely that an ordinary dog from the Southland would have died from such brutality. Then White Fang is securely chained, and soon afterward Gray Beaver departs from Fort Yukon, leaving White Fang as the sole property of Beauty Smith.

In these and in the following scenes, London is giving us a picture of the ultimate depravity of human nature, and of the indignities that White Fang must endure in order that London can picture the contrast later with the gentle and humane treatment which White Fang will receive from Weedon Scott.

The lowest ebb of White Fang's fortunes are now presented. He is the property of a vicious and cruel master who uses him only for savage and vicious purposes. The reader should be reminded that Beauty Smith bought White Fang because White Fang was a beast which could fulfill Smith's hatred toward his fellow human beings. Thus, he uses the dog cruelly, and he makes much money betting on White Fang to win fights against other dogs; yet whereas earlier White Fang had hated only members of his own kind, now White Fang is imbued with a hatred toward everything that *leaves* him. Eventually, he develops such a reputation as a fighter that on one occasion a fight promoter even throws a lynx into a cage with him. At another time, two dogs are thrown into the ring at the same time, and White Fang, while victorious, is almost killed in the contest.

After some time, when there are no other people willing to pit a dog against White Fang, there appears a "Faro-dealer," a man named Tim Keenan, who arrives with the first bulldog ever to enter the territory of the North.

In White Fang's encounter between Cherokee, the bulldog, they, at first, do not even want to fight. Neither dog has ever seen anything like the other. Finally, however, Tim Keenan is able to coax the bulldog into stalking White Fang. The contest, then, is between the quickness of White Fang, as opposed to the steadfast determination and mechanical jaws of the bulldog, and White Fang becomes confused because he leaps forward and bites the bulldog, and yet the bulldog seems not to be distracted from his constant and deliberate stalking of White Fang. In spite of White Fang's constant and clever maneuvers, he is unable to reach the tough, loose-skinned, well protected throat of the bulldog, who continues to pursue White Fang. During one attack, White Fang, for the first time in his life, loses his footing, and the bulldog is able to grab the lower part of White Fang's throat. Once the bulldog's jaws have closed upon White Fang's throat, nothing can seemingly loosen the bulldog's vice-like grip. There seems to be no escaping the grip. White Fang, to all appearances, is at the point of death. Beauty Smith, in an attempt to provoke White Fang's wrath, begins to laugh derisively at White Fang, and, once more, White Fang makes a great effort to free himself from the bulldog, but the vice-like jaws of Cherokee are locked too tightly.

At this point, the crowd suddenly gives way to two men who appear on the scene. Because betting on arranged dog fights is illegal, the crowd assumes immediately that these two men are associated, somehow, with the civil authorities. Only Beauty Smith attempts to stop the men from ending the dog fight, but he is quickly knocked away, yet these two men are still unable to separate the two dogs, and one of the men, Weedon Scott, calls for his friend, Matt, to place a gun between the bulldog's teeth and pry the dog's jaws open. Then, once they have extracted White Fang's mangled neck from Cherokee's jaws, it is discovered that White Fang is, indeed, nearly dead, yet he is still breathing. Weedon Scott then instructs Tim Keenan to take his bulldog away, and he gives Beauty Smith one hundred and fifty dollars for White Fang. When Beauty Smith tries to protest, Weedon Scott reminds Beauty Smith that he could have him arrested if he makes any trouble.

With the appearance of Weedon Scott, we have a total contrast with Beauty Smith. White Fang, however, has almost been driven mad by Beauty Smith's wickedness and maltreatment. Thus, at the beginning of White Fang's relationship with Weedon Scott, White Fang can feel nothing but hatred and contempt for *all* living human beings. It will take a great deal of patience on the part of Weedon Scott to transform White Fang from a wild savage dog into a civilized dog. This, of course, will be the concern of the rest of the novel.

When Weedon Scott and his friend, Matt, return to their cabin with White Fang, they are, at first, unsuccessful in calming the dog, and White Fang has to be chained. For two weeks, the men examine the dog and discuss his merit. They notice certain signs that indicate that he seems to have been, at one time, a dog trained for the harness, and they both realize that he is a dog of great intelligence. It is decided, finally, that they will take a chance and unchain White Fang and see what happens. When Matt throws White Fang a piece of meat, another dog, Major, jumps at it, and White Fang immediately kills Major. Incensed, Matt attempts to kick White Fang, but instead, Matt is bitten in the leg by White Fang. Weedon Scott is ready to kill White Fang, but Matt convinces him that it was Matt's own fault that the dog bit him. When Weedon Scott approaches White Fang in an attempt to pet him, White Fang instinctively recoils and bites Scott in the hand. At this point, Matt comes out with a rifle, planning to shoot the dog. Seeing the gun, White Fang immediately hides behind the house, an act which convinces Scott and Matt of White Fang's supreme intelligence and civilized ways. Thus, they decide not to kill White Fang because "he's got intelligence, and we've got to give that intelligence a chance." Yet whereas Gray Beaver was not actually cruel to White Fang, Weedon Scott and Matt are the first compassionate people whom White Fang has ever encountered; thus, since Weedon Scott is determined to tame White Fang, he proceeds to do so by bringing White Fang chunks of meat and offering them to the dog. At first, though, White Fang does not sufficiently trust Scott enough to come and take the meat from his hand. But after some time, and also some patience on Scott's part, White Fang gradually learns to take meat from Scott's hand. Later on, when Weedon Scott attempts to pat White Fang on the head and shoulders, it is "distasteful to [White Fang's] instinct," and yet he finally allows the man to do so, even though he growls while he is being petted.

"It was the beginning," says London, of a new life for White Fang, and it was the "ending of the old life and the reign of hate." Whereas White Fang had shown allegiance and loyalty to Gray Beaver, White Fang now feels growing within him a liking for Scott, and soon an affection for him, and finally a deep love for the man. As the days pass, White Fang's affection for Weedon Scott grows, and London tells us that "it was necessary that he [White Fang] should have some god. The lordship of man was a need of his nature." Ultimately, then, White Fang comes to tolerate even Matt, who is given the task of feeding him. But all of White Fang's loyalty and love is reserved for Weedon Scott alone. For example, when Matt tries to harness White

Fang, he is unable to do so, yet White Fang allows Weedon Scott to place him in the harness, and White Fang becomes the leader of a dog team which both respects and admires him.

It is a custom of White Fang's to wait up for Scott to return to the cabin every night, and once, when Scott has to go away on a long journey, White Fang refuses to eat or even move from the cabin. He finally is on the point of dying when Weedon Scott returns, but within two and a half days, White Fang regains his strength and health. One night, not long afterward, Weedon Scott and Matt hear White Fang attack something outside, and upon investigating, they discover that White Fang has pinned down a man. It is Beauty Smith who has come back with a club and a chain, hoping to be able to steal White Fang.

In Part Four, then, London shows the wild, fierce, savage, and ferocious wolf being transformed by the healing power of love, represented by Weedon Scott. London seems to imply that any animal's psychology can be soothed if the animal is treated properly. The closing scene of this section, with the reappearance of the savage and cruel Beauty Smith, seems to imply that savage treatment evokes savagery and hatred, whereas love and compassionate treatment evoke loyalty and devotion.

Part Five

This section of the novel presents the final changes that will take place within White Fang. Beginning with Part Two, when we saw White Fang as a young puppy, we have followed him from being a creature of the wild to becoming a part of civilization.

At the beginning of Part Five, White Fang senses that there is going to be a change. We find out that Weedon Scott is planning to return to his home in the Southland – Sierra Vista, California. Since Weedon Scott had left White Fang for a short time in Part Four, White Fang is intelligent enough now to know that his master is about to leave him again. Both Weedon Scott and Matt agree that it will be totally impossible to take a wild wolf back to live in the civilization of the Southland. They assume that he would be impossible to domesticate. Thus, when they leave the cabin, they lock the front door, and Matt goes out the back door, locking it. White Fang is left inside. As the two men head down to the boat, they hear White Fang howling, as though "his master was dead." He is "voicing utter woe. His cry [burst] upward in great heartbreaking rushes, dying down into quavering misery. . . ."

When Weedon Scott boards his homeward-bound ship, he finds White Fang sitting on the deck of the ship. Upon examining the animal, Matt and Weedon Scott decide that White Fang must have broken through the window in the cabin in order to follow his master. Realizing anew the degree of devotion which White Fang has for him, Scott decides to take the animal with him to the Southland despite the fact that he believes that the dog will never be able to become civilized, much less endure the hot climate.

When he arrives in San Francisco, White Fang feels as though he is experiencing some type of nightmare. He is bombarded by strange sounds, sounds of the city, and he is overwhelmed by the sight of all of the tall buildings and crowded streets. He is completely bewildered. He then has to endure being chained in the baggage car, his only consolation being that he can see and smell his master's luggage, which he will not allow anyone to approach.

Arriving at Sierra Vista, Scott embraces his mother, which causes White Fang to become a "snarling, raging demon." When White Fang is reprimanded by his master, he is finally satisfied that the woman is not going to hurt Scott. This, however, is only the beginning of many experiences which White Fang will have to undergo until he becomes domesticated. Fortunately, White Fang has sufficient intelligence to totally obey Weedon Scott's commands. When they arrive at the Scott estate, for example, they are greeted by a large sheep-dog named Collie, who tries to attack White Fang immediately upon seeing him. White Fang instinctively knows, though, that this is a female of the species, so he turns his shoulder and shunts her attacks. The sheep-dog, out of an ancient instinct, knows that this wolf is a natural enemy to her position as a protective sheep-dog. Thus, Collie, the sheep-dog, is introduced to us as the antagonist of White Fang, and her attack upon him will continue for some time. In fact, she will be the main bane of White Fang's existence for some time. This is ironic because the novel will end with White Fang going off into the forest with the sheep-dog in order to mate with her and thus begin a new breed of dog.

Upon their arrival at the house, a dog named Dick runs to greet Weedon Scott, and White Fang instinctively feels that his master is being attacked, and again he is prepared to kill. And he would have done so, had not Collie hit White Fang from the side and broke the line of his attack, which allows Weedon Scott time enough to stop the fight. Weedon knows that White Fang could have easily killed Dick.

After his first introduction to the estate, White Fang has a series of things which he has to learn. For example, the dog Dick would like to be friends with White Fang, but for too long in his life, White Fang has been adverse to friendships of any kind. Compared to the things that White Fang has to learn at Sierra Vista, life in the Northland was a very simple affair. For example, in the Northland, all that White Fang had to learn was that Mit-sah and Kloo-kooch belonged to Gray Beaver. However, in Sierra Vista, relationships are infinitely more complicated. In addition to all of the various members of Weedon Scott's family—mother, father, wife, two sisters, and two children—there are numerous servants and workers. Furthermore, White Fang has always disliked children, but now he has to learn to like Scott's children, even though they pull his fur and hit him.

Moreover, White Fang cannot fight with any of the other dogs. The only domesticated animals in the North were dogs, and White Fang could attack them. But here in the Southland, White Fang cannot even kill the chickens—or any other domesticated animal. (After White Fang *has*, however, killed some chickens, Weedon Scott makes a bet with his father, that after Scott commands White Fang *not* to kill another chicken, that White Fang can be placed within the chicken coop itself, and that he will not touch another chicken. Weeden Scott is correct.)

Being intelligent, White Fang quickly learns that between him and all domesticated animals (cats, rabbits, turkeys, sheep, and goats), there must be *no hostility*. However, when he is out on the land with Weedon Scott, the creatures of the wild are lawful prey. Still, however, life is very complex in the valley for White Fang. For example, there are butcher shops, where fresh meat is hanging, but White Fang cannot eat it; children throw stones at him, and he can do nothing; and, in addition, tame dogs chase him, but he is not allowed to kill them.

One day, however, some men in a saloon urge their dogs to attack White Fang, and Weedon Scott tells White Fang to "eat 'em up." White Fang immediately kills two of the dogs, and another tries to escape, but White Fang chases it across a field and kills it. After that, the men of the town keep their dogs away from White Fang.

As the months go by, White Fang comes to enjoy the prosperous and indulgent life that he leads, but he remains at a distance from the other animals – except for the "one trial in his life" – Collie. She never gives White Fang a moment of peace. Otherwise, things go well.

When Weedon Scott goes for long horseback rides, sometimes up to fifty miles a day, White Fang enjoys accompanying his master. He never tires, even after the longest trips. Then one day, a rabbit frightens Weedon Scott's horse, causing the horse to stumble, and this accident causes Weedon to break a leg. Scott then tells White Fang to go home and get help. White Fang is very reluctant to leave his master, and it is with great difficulty that Scott finally convinces the dog to leave him and go to the ranch for help. Once at the ranch, however, White Fang's problems have just begun. He cannot communicate with the other members of the Scott family. And the more he tries, the more they are convinced that White Fang has gone berserk. For only the second time in his life, in desperation, White Fang makes himself *bark*. But, by doing so, he finally makes himself understood, and Weedon is soon rescued. After this, White Fang is more respected by the other members of the Scott family.

As the days continue, White Fang gradually realizes that Collie's bites are becoming more playful and flirtatious. When she "nipped his ear," White Fang realizes that it is an invitation for him to follow her, in the same way that, long years ago, his mother followed old One Eye into the forest.

In the final chapter of the novel, White Fang performs a feat which causes him to be called the "Blessed Wolf." It seems that years ago, Judge Scott had sentenced a criminal, Jim Hall, to fifty years in prison. Even though this criminal, Jim Hall, had been guilty of two earlier offenses, he was innocent of *this* offense, and he had been framed by the police.

As a result, Jim Hall believes that Judge Scott is a part of the conspiracy. Thus, when Judge Scott sentences him to fifty years in prison, Hall threatens to get his revenge – eventually – on the Judge. Years pass and, meanwhile, Jim Hall becomes a thoroughly hardened criminal, mainly because of his brutal treatment while in prison. But while he is in solitary confinement, he manages to escape, killing three guards while doing so.

When the Scott family hears about Hall's escape, everyone except the Judge is frightened. The Judge's wife, Alice, secretly goes downstairs every night and lets White Fang in so that he can sleep in the hallway. But since White Fang is not allowed in the house (by the Judge), Judge Scott's wife has to get up early each morning and let White Fang out. Consequently, on the night that Jim Hall silently breaks into the Judge's home, White Fang is there, and just as the convict is ascending the stairs, White Fang attacks him and quickly kills him. White Fang, however, is seriously wounded himself during the combat, and Judge Scott wires San Francisco for the very best doctor who can be found – a Doctor Nichols. Any other dog would have died, but because White Fang is a wolf-dog, his constitution is different, and he survives.

After this episode, Alice Scott names White Fang the "Blessed Wolf," a name which he retains for the rest of his life. When at last the Scotts bring the Blessed Wolf home from the hospital, White Fang, in his weakened condition, is taken outside so that he can see the puppies which he has fathered. As the puppies come sprawling over him, "he lay with half-shut patient eyes drowsing in the sun."

CRITICAL THEORIES

Jack London did not adhere to any particular philosophical or critical theories. Instead, he fluctuated from one critical view to another as the moment seemed to warrant it. Perfect proof of this statement lies in the fact that *The Call of the Wild* (1903) shows the Darwinian theories of the "survival of the fittest," as a dog is taken from its civilized Southland and is placed in the primitive North, where it must learn to cope with all sorts of primitive conditions if it is to survive. Then only three years later, London was to write the antithesis to this story in *White Fang* (1906), showing how a wild animal of the North (three-fourths wolf) who has been severely mistreated can, through a change in environment and proper attention, be changed into a civilized animal of the Southland.

When Jack London was born in 1876, Charles Darwin's theories of evolution dominated the scientific and theological world, and London utilized many of Darwin's theories in his writings. Essentially, this theory of evolution investigated the sources from which modern man developed and tried to describe how modern man was a result of a long period of evolution from other organisms (the most popular theory concerns the concept that somewhere back in time, both man and ape-like animals were descended from a common ancestor). During this process of evolution, all living things were subjected to a process known as "natural selection," which means that only those species which are the most adaptable to any given place or environment are able to survive. Accordingly, we have the concept of the "survival of the fittest." This is one of the dominant concepts in *The Call of the Wild* and also in *White Fang*. For example, of all the dogs that are taken to the Great North, only Buck is able to make the transition completely – because he is the strongest and the most determined to survive. The *instinct to survive* is the strongest instinct known to man or animal. Likewise, in *White Fang*, the only cub of the five in the litter to survive is White Fang – again because of the "survival of the fittest" theory and, by implication, the elimination of the weakest. Consequently, in these two novels and in other works by London, the idea of a struggle for survival among hostile or unknown forces is one of the dominant concepts found in the novels. The ability of the "animal" or "person" to adapt to new and different surroundings constitutes the essential plot of such novels.

Another concept which influenced London's writing was a method of writing called Naturalism. This involves both a technique and a way of viewing life. Essentially, the literary concept of Naturalism grew out of the concept of Realism during the latter part of the nineteenth century. The realist had wanted to "hold up a mirror to life" and to render a very accurate picture of life. The naturalist wanted to go a step further and examine life as a scientist would. Thus, the technique of the naturalist involves viewing life with scientific objectivity. Throughout his novels, London tries to depict his scenes in the great North with the objectivity of a scientist. He had personally been present in this Yukon country, and in scenes like the opening part of *White Fang*, he is able to capture the pure essence of the great frozen North, with all of its challenges to life.

More important, for the naturalist, man is controlled by basic urges, and he can do very little to determine his own destiny. Forces of environment, heredity, and biological instincts combine to control man's life. These basic and elemental urges place man in a position similar to that of animals. Consequently, according to the naturalist, man can, at any moment, resort to animal instinct or animal behavior, and thus London chose to write about animals, showing them resorting, at key times, to the primitive behavior that is in their own makeup.

A man or an animal born in one type of environment is influenced accordingly – to a point where the basic actions in his life are governed by these environmental forces. Carried to an extreme, this view of life leads to determinism – that is, the idea that man (or animal) can do nothing for himself or itself and is, therefore, at the mercy of forces outside of his own self. Consequently, White Fang and Buck are molded by their early environment and during the course of each novel, each dog has to change drastically in order to continue to function in a new and different environment.

Furthermore, man and animal are the victims of their elemental drives, which are, in turn, motivated by their environment, the biological need to survive, and by the hereditary traits of the characters. For example, when Buck is placed in the great North, his first instinct is to survive in this new and different environment. The biological need to survive influences the actions of both Buck and White Fang during the earliest parts of both novels. Likewise, the hereditary traits in Buck's makeup have lain dormant for generations, but during the course of the novel, he begins to hear the primitive "call of the wild," which arouses a deep instinctual urge in him and forces him, finally, to answer the various calls of the wild. As a result, he finally resorts to the primitive forces that have lain dormant in him. In contrast, White Fang is primitive, but since he possesses some part of the tame dog, the wolf part of his psyche is able to respond to human compassion and love, and thus he is able to finally function within a civilized society.

London also used other current concepts in his writing and even in the use of the above concepts, he was not always consistent. For example, while being very "naturalistic" in his philosophy, some of his chapters in *The Call of the Wild* touch upon a very romantic strain, evoking a desire in all of us for the romantic desire to escape from civilization and return to our primitive natures. It is the combination of these various ideas that causes London's fiction to be so appealing to such a large number of readers.

QUESTIONS FOR REVIEW

1. Trace White Fang's development from a puppy to a fully grown animal.

2. Trace White Fang's change from a domineering, vicious animal of the wild to that of a totally civilized animal.

3. Compare and/or contrast White Fang's three masters – that is, Gray Beaver, Beauty Smith, and Weedon Scott.

4. How is the idea of the "survival of the fittest" used throughout this novel?

5. Since Part One of the novel takes place before White Fang is born, justify the inclusion of this part of the novel, dealing with the episode of Henry and Bill, who are never heard from or seen again in the course of the novel.

6. Compare and/or contrast life in the Northland to that of life in the Southland.

7. Discuss the various uses by London of anthropomorphism – that is, the assigning of human qualities to non-humans.

SELECTED BIBLIOGRAPHY

BROOKS, VAN WYCK. *Sketches in Criticism.* (1932).

FONER, PHILIP S. *Jack London, American Rebel.* (1947).

JACK LONDON NEWSLETTER (Vol. 1, No. 1 – present). Carbondale: Southern Illinois University Library. (There are numerous articles throughout the series both on *The Call of the Wild* and *White Fang.*)

LONDON, JACK. *John Barleycorn.* (1913). (Contains many autobiographical entries.)

POWERS, RICHARD G. *The Science Fiction of Jack London.* (1975).

SINCLAIR, ANDREW. *Jack: A Biography of Jack London.* (1978).

WALCUTT, CHARLES C. *American Literary Naturalism: A Divided Stream.* (1956).